Behind the

My Life with Rock and Roll Legends

By Scott Cahill and Galen Senogles

~~~

Published by Scott Cahill and Galen Senogles

Copyright 2013 Scott Cahill and Galen Senogles

Edited by Rick Barclay and Scott Pullman

Printed by CreateSpace, An Amazon.com Company
Available from Amazon.com and other retail outlets

Available on Kindle and online stores

Available at smashwords.com

All rights reserved

ISBN-13:978-1495347597

DEDICATION

This book is dedicated to:

Mom and Dad

Glen Willard Senogles and Laurine Marie Senogles

Special thanks to:

Galen Duke Senogles

Table of Contents

Beginning

Dedication

Forward

Behind the Board: My Life with Rock and Roll Legends

Forward

I am Willie Leacox, the drummer with the band "America," and have been the drummer for them for forty years give or take. In my early days, I played with many bands, many of whom I have forgotten about completely and a bunch of musicians I certainly have no memory of. But of all those bands I played with I would have to say that the most instrumental band in getting me to where I am today was "The Jerms," spelled with a "J." Our motto was, "WE WILL INFECT YOUR AREA SOON!"

Most of us were college students at Washburn University in Topeka, Kansas, where I received my Bachelors of Music Education (BME). We 'gigged' mostly on weekends, college holidays, and lengthy summer tours. The Christmas break in 1969 found us in Nashville, Tennessee, recording our single, "Green Door," which made it all the way to number 98 on the Billboard top 100 chart. This got us the gig to open for the legendary band, Three Dog Night in their up and coming summer tour.

Unfortunately, my time in the band was short as I had to leave "The Jerms" to stay in college and keep my student deferment. This kept me from being drafted into the military and being sent to Vietnam. I enjoyed my time with "The Jerms" and with Galen. I look back at those days fondly and have many great memories. I have a lot of my own stories about playing with the Jerms as well, but I think I will let Galen tell you about the many, wild experiences in his own words. Enjoy the tour of this book.

-Willie Leacox, longtime drummer for Grammy Award Winning Band "America" and former drummer for the Jerms.

Behind the Board:
My Life with Rock and Roll Legends

The world of music is filled with a litany of close calls, near misses, brushes with fame, and filled with enough what-ifs, what-could-have-beens, and any number of alternate history scenarios that could have changed the face of the musical landscape as we know it. Our story is one in the same vein; a kid from Kansas whose brush with fame brought him working side by side with some of music's most iconic figures. With an early opportunity squandered and given instead to Simon and Garfunkel, to later playing concert dates with the likes of The Yardbirds, Three Dog Night, Jefferson Airplane, Steppenwolf, and other rock legends; and later working side by side in the production room with the likes of Fleetwood Mac, Pink Floyd, members of The Beatles, Steely Dan and other members of rock and roll royalty.

This is the true story that serves as a musical stepping-stone and sidebar notation that, while on one hand provides evidence of some of rock's most enduring rumors and legends, dispels and disproves with the other. This work is sure to create a whole new genre of debate and discussion in musical history spanning the early Sixties through the advent of classic rock, disco, and the advent of rap and modern music as we know it.

*****

SC: Take us all the way back...what was your story? Where did you grow up and how did you first develop your interest in music?

GS: I grew up in Topeka, Kansas of all places. Later on, I realized how—had I been out to either the East or West Coast instead of the Midwest—my music career would have been vastly different, but we can get into that later and as I tell some of the other stories, it will probably make a lot more sense. The closest I came—as a musician—to playing the bigger cities was playing in Chicago at a place called the Rush Up. Once again, though, we can get into that later.

SC: Did you always have an interest in music? Did you take piano lessons or have any of the other types of experiences that some musicians have as far as their first taste of music?

GS: Not at all. As a matter of fact, I was always one of the top students in school, and one of the first things I remember wanting to do as a career was to be a math teacher. It was something I always excelled at. It wasn't until later that I learned that both music and math share some of the same properties, so it wasn't hard to figure my interest in music. I was on the debate team, an honor student, and in the top 1% scholastically. In those days, I was a nerdish kind of brainy-type of kid getting 4.0 grades.

SC: What was the pivotal moment where you realized you wanted to try and play music, or get into the field?

GS: It was a long time ago, Scott, so through the 60s and 70s—trust me—my memory isn't as sharp as it probably could be, and I already sound enough like Joe Walsh. That said, I would have to say it was like almost every other kid who wanted to play in the 60s: seeing the Beatles on Ed Sullivan. I remember watching and thinking, "Oh my

God! This is what I want to do." My older brother was into Elvis and all that stuff, so when I saw The Beatles, it changed my life. Then, we started our band and we started getting all of the girls, which made it better. The very first song I learned to play was The Beatles version of "Twist and Shout."

SC: Well, you are in good company; I know Gene Simmons and Steven Van Zandt both spoke of how watching the Ed Sullivan performances was the key moment in time that drew them to music.

GS: I never heard that about Gene Simmons, but I'm not surprised at all. I remember watching The Beatles in that living room in Kansas and it opened a door that I had never thought about until then. I asked my dad to buy me a guitar. He did the next best thing: he went out into the garage and made me one.

SC: So, as opposed to buying a guitar out of the Sears catalog or hitting up the pawn shop, your dad went out and simply built you a guitar?

GS: I owe so much to my father and my parents. Him building that guitar for me was just one of many things my parents did for me. I think my dad's interest in building things also spurned me somewhat. I was one of the first to try and build effects units and fuzz boxes. I really loved the technology aspect of being a musician. I am pretty sure I owned one of the first Danelectro's in the US, and know for sure that I was one of the first in the US to play a Marshall Amp.

SC: What?

GS: Yeah, to the best of my knowledge, I was one the first to order a Marshall Amp from England and have it shipped into the US.

SC: Do you remember what happened to it?

GS: I had some amazing gear back in the day, but sold a lot of it. It was the ups and downs of being in the industry, and I was always in the moment and didn't really plan for the future like I should have. In the mid-60s, I was handling all of the money from our tours, and we were taking in a couple thousand a night for each show. So, I had the money to buy the best equipment.

This photo was used for the cover of The Jerms first 45 single "Good Feelin Yea", and "Bald Headed Women". The 45 was released in 1965 and was a regional hit. The record was sent to Columbia Records and landed The Jerms a record deal.

SC: Let's not get too far ahead of ourselves here. What was your band and how did it get started?

GS: After seeing The Beatles, and my dad making me a guitar, I was still split between music and going to school. I did advanced courses and extra course work, which allowed me to graduate at 16 years old. I got a scholarship at Washburn University in Kansas for my math skills. At this time, thanks to The Beatles and whatnot, I was growing my hair long, which is short by today's standards.

SC: So, being the young, smart kid with semi-long hair probably wasn't easy at a Midwest school in the mid-60s?

GS: Yeah, it was the first time I heard someone say to me, "Is he a boy or a girl?" and that was a comment I probably heard a thousand times over the next couple of years.

SC: Go back, then. What was the name of your band and when did that start?

GS: In the mid-60s, I started a band in the Midwest called, "The Jerms."

SC: Not to be confused with 80s punk band "The Germs" right?

GS: Yeah, we spelled our name with a J instead of the G. We were maybe the best, most popular band in the Midwest. As a matter of fact, that was our first brush with fame.

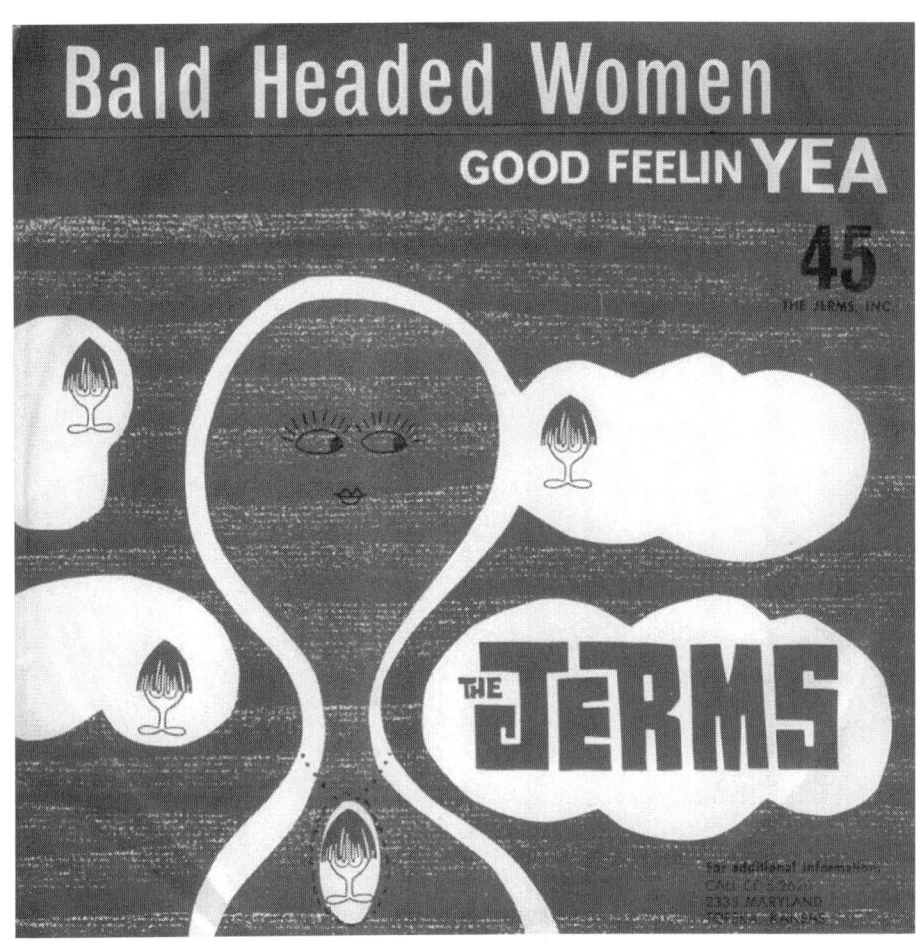

The Jerms 45 single cover for "Bald Headed Woman" released by The Jerms in 1964.

The Jerms 45 single cover for "Good Feelin Yea" released by The Jerms in 1964.

We were making a name of ourselves and had recorded a few 45s. Back then, there were only four or five companies putting out records, so I sent a 45 to each of the studios. One night, I got a call from a guy named Bob Johnston. At first, I thought it was a friend playing a joke, but it was Bob Johnston from Columbia Records. At that time, he was producing [Bob] Dylan. He said that he wanted to offer us a contract to come out to New York to record and be promoted and all of that stuff. A few days later, we all received contracts and a full itinerary of shows, appearances, and tours. In those days as well, the record companies would have studio musicians record the instruments and let the lead singer record the vocals.

SC: So, at that time you were on the verge of being discovered and potentially being the next big thing?

GS: Yeah. I remember looking at the schedule and they had us in the studio at a certain time as well as a schedule of promotional appearances, and some tours we were scheduled to go on. All of us signed the contract except our lead singer, whose parents got involved and were making changes to the contract and hired a lawyer. There was some bantering and negotiations back and forth, and finally I got a letter a couple of months later that said, "Due to problems with contract negotiation, all offers made by Columbia are null and void," or some other legalese. I'll never forget it. They were squabbling over 3% and 5%. The letter actually said that Columbia was offering the contract meant for the Jerms to the next act on the list—which happened to be Simon and Garfunkel.

SC: That is amazing! Your lead singer's parents in Podunk, Kansas try to play hardball with Columbia Records to the point where the record company cancels the offer altogether, and instead of The Jerms being promoted nationally, the big break ends up going to Simon and Garfunkel?

GS: That's exactly what happened. I think Columbia signed Paul Revere and the Raiders as well. We went back to Kansas, paid the lawyer we hired, and forgot about it for a while.

SC: What year was all this taking place?

GS: I would think this was around the end of 1965 or so. I was listening to Rubber Soul and Revolver around that time so 1965 or 1966 would be my best guess. After that whole incident, I fired the lead singer and started taking on more vocals and decided to make all band decisions after that. I still think about what could have been, and how things may have been different, but at the same time, still loved the music and being in a band, so I kept going with it.

SC: What happened to the lead singer after that?

GS: He borrowed my brother's motorcycle, was involved in a serious crash, and never played again.

SC: So, you are 16 years old in Kansas and just turned down from Columbia Records. Was it back to high school?

GS: Well, at that time, I still had really good grades and graduated high school early. So between playing music and gigs, I started college at 16. It was Washburn University, which was a university school in Kansas.

SC: I bet you are the youngest kid in school, with long hair...that must have been tough, right?

GS: Oh yeah! I'll never forget my first day. I walked into the classroom and this professor calls my name for roll call and then looks at me and says, "You look like a troublemaker." I just look at him and [say something] like "What?" and he says, "Look at your hair—you must be a fucking troublemaker."

SC: As a 16 year-old, it probably shocked you that professors could say stuff like that, right?

GS: Yeah. I was an honor student and kind of respected in high school, and here I am a couple of months later being cussed out because of my hair. After that, I got up from my seat and un-enrolled from all of my classes. I went home locked myself in my room and just started writing songs. Then, the band started growing, and at 17, I re-enrolled back in school.

SC: Was this still Washburn?

GS: Yeah. I was older and more prepared. By that time, the popularity of The Beatles had softened up the acceptance for long hair.

SC: So, by then, longer hair was more trendy in other words?

GS: Oh yeah. More people were doing their own thing and whatnot.

I remember, though, sitting on the grass in front of the school, when a bunch of the football team surrounded me and set in with the, "Is he a boy or a girl?" routine. Little did they know, the week before, I was playing a gig in Nebraska, and I was filling up the gas tank. One of the things I always did was fill up the tank—no matter where I was—because in the Midwest, you were driving hundreds of miles and never knew if the gas stations were open or not.

Anyhow, I am filling up the tank when a bunch of Hells' Angels pull in. One of the guys gets off his bike and walks up to me and says, "You want to go to a party tonight?" Being that there are 20 or so bikers, I was like, "If you want me to go, I guess I can go." And then—I will never forget this—he grabs me by the collar and kisses me on the lips and says to me "You're welcome." So I attended a Hells' Angels party in the middle of Nebraska. Funny enough about a week later, there were some football players were getting ready to beat me up because of my hair.

So, I stand up and walk over to the guy with the biggest mouth who was doing the most talking, grab him by the scruff, kissed him square on the lips and said, "Let's do it baby." They were all so confused! After that, they all left me alone. That little Hells' Angels trick probably saved me from getting my ass kicked, but that was the type of stuff we dealt with all of the time back then.

SC: What was college like?

GS: It was much smoother the second time. Oddly enough, the only professor who gave me a hard time was the music teacher. He told me, "You're not serious and you're not going to do well in my class, and I don't want you in my class." I ended up getting an A because it was in that class that I realized a lot of the principles of math also applied to music, so I was able to easily write three-part harmonies and things like that. He (the professor) came up to me at the end of the semester and apologized to me, so that was really cool.

I learned a lot more theory and a bit of piano here and there. I think I learned "Go Now" by The Moody Blues and "Summer in the City." So, music started becoming the dominant thing. Instead of just doing music on the weekends, I started doing it weeknights as well. School was going great, as I was getting straight-A's in mathematics, and even the minor courses like theology and religion and those type of courses, but music was becoming more dominant day-to-day.

SC: Did you get your degree?

GS: No, I made the decision to do music full time, and at that point, dropped everything else.

SC: Were your parents shocked when you got home and told them you were dropping out of school to play in a rock band?

GS: My parents were always supportive of me. They said go for it. "If that's what you want to do, we support you one hundred percent."

SC: So, you lived in Kansas; did you live on a farm? Did your Dad work in a grain mill or something like that?

GS: My dad actually worked for the newspaper we had in the city, which was *The Topeka Capital-Journal*. My uncle was well known as one of top watercolor artists, so we had people in the family who were artists and creative and all that stuff.

SC: Okay, so you decided to become a full time musician. What happened then?

GS: From that point, we were on the road. Day and night, we were on the road.

SC: Let me ask you—before we get into that—did you have a manager, or was it you calling to set up gigs? How was setting up tours and making arrangements and all of that stuff handled?

GS: When it started, they would call us. They would call my dad's home phone because of our records and all that. Then, we got a booking agency out of Lawrence, Kansas who started booking us gigs. Days, nights, anytime, everywhere—Wyoming, New Mexico, everywhere in the Midwest…We were considered the number-one band in the Midwest, so [we] had a lot of popularity. We were pretty good.

SC: I remember you said you played rhythm guitar?

GS: Yeah, I played rhythm and a bit of lead here and there. I also sang all of John Lennon's parts as well as any Dylan songs we were playing then. That was my thing: I was the John and the Bob of the band. I never really thought I was a good singer, so the Bob Dylan songs made sense [*laughs*]. That's when the touring stories really begin. Our agency hired Wolfman Jack to advertise us on his show, so we got hired to do all sorts of schools and parties.

SC: Wolfman Jack was a supporter?

GS: No, but we paid him to talk about our band and he did.

SC: Do you remember what he got paid?

GS: I'm not sure, because it was paid for by agency fees....probably $20 bucks or something. Wolfman would say stuff like, "This is the Wolfman from Del Rio, Texas, and The Jerms will be playing in Bellview, Nebraska on August 10th at the Municipal Auditorium." Back then, that was the best advertising you could get, and it paid seeing as almost all of our gigs were full.

SC: So the Wolfman helped fill a bunch of dates?

GS: Yeah, and more dates meant it was a whole lot of driving. As the leader of the band and having no trust in the other band members—whom I thought were a bunch of idiots—it basically was me doing all of the driving to all of our gigs in the Midwest.

We had a big, old Cadillac and a trailer that we would use to haul our gear. I used to take black beauties to help keep me up, and that was the start of eight-track tapes. So, a stack of Beatles eight-tracks and some black beauties, and I was on my way. We would drive all night long and we started to develop a kinship with the truckers. We knew all of the signals and hand signs. It was the late Sixties, and this was really when the fun began with parties and girls.

SC: So this is where the story gets psychedelic?

GS: Oh yeah. Acid and other drugs were starting to become more popular. I never liked acid, though, as I always want to be able to come down when I want to come down, and acid generally didn't allow that option. So, I did it a couple of times, but it never became my thing.

SC: Share some road stories with us.

GS: We opened up for The Yardbirds.

SC: No kidding? What era of The Yardbirds was it?

GS: I think it was around '66, so probably the era with Jeff Beck, I'm guessing. The gig was in Oklahoma City, and we stayed with them at the Holiday Inn. We also played with Steppenwolf, Three Dog Night, and Jefferson Airplane.

SC: Tell me some stories about The Yardbirds.

GS: They were cool. The hotel was flooded with girls, and we helped them out by taking the extra girls that they weren't interested in [*laughs*].

SC: Do you have any recollections about hanging with them specifically and talking about guitars or music or anything?

GS: I just remember it was a huge party all of the time.

SC: So you never talked music or gear with Jeff Beck or Jimmy Page?

GS: No, but I remember after we finished opening up for them and clearing our stuff off the stage, we would watch from the side and think, "I will never be as good as these guys. I should quit now. What am I doing here? I don't even belong on the same stage as these guys."

You know, but I belonged to the same party [*laughs*]. Remember, as well: this was before AIDS and whatnot, so back then, the worse thing you would get was gonorrhea.

I remember after the Oklahoma City gig, we had to drive to Silver City, New Mexico. In those days, the speed limit was 90 miles per hour. After driving all night long, sun's coming up and all that—I had to go down this huge, long hill to get into the city.

So, I am going 90 miles per hour, down this hill, with a trailer full of equipment, and just wanting to rest, when this car pulls out from a side street right in front of us. I slam on the brakes, and the Caddie and the trailer are swerving all over the road sideways and all this stuff. We flipped the driver off, and I think some of the band mooned them or something, because I am thinking, "You fuckers almost killed us!" and we were like one-inch from death.

Anyhow, we pull into a gas station because I always filled the tank at every stop, and next thing I know we are surrounded by cops with their guns drawn and cars and everything. One of the cops walks up to me and right in my face says, "You were the one who embarrassed my wife by giving us the fingers and mooning us. You are going to jail."

So, they cuff us and parade us down to the city jail. They throw us each in a different cell. The commode in the cell I was in had so much green mold on it that I was actually afraid to pee in it. During the time I'm in the cell, this huge drunken, American Indian lady comes in fighting with six cops, and she is throwing them around like rag dolls. It was insanity.

Anyhow, they bring me to face the sheriff, so I request my phone call. I call my attorney and explain the story, and he (the attorney) says on the other end of the line, "I can't help you, there is nothing I can I do. Humor them." So, I am on the other end of the line, and I say out loud so the sheriff can hear, "So you're going to take care of it? Thank you! Thank you so much! I really appreciate it." The sheriff says, "You had your call—get back into your cell."

About an hour later, he comes back and says, "We've got a problem: you guys are *not* playing tonight and the local kids are rioting. We are going to sneak you out the back door to the next county and we have a judge who is going to try you right then and there on the spot." I was just happy to be out of jail, though I was worried what would happen. We ended up in this old guy's house. He was some old retired judge from New Orleans, and we are standing in front of him and the cops tell their side of the story.

Then, we tell our side of the story, and this old judge just starts laughing his ass off and says, "That's the best story I have heard in years! I'm going to fine you (each band member) $5 bucks, and don't let us ever catch you in this town again."

We later got a copy of the local newspaper that did a story saying, "Justice was served as four long-haired hippies were arrested on counts of lewd behavior." I think that was the same tour we saw a dead cow on the side of the road, and stopped to take off the horns and tie them to the front of the Caddie. We were all wearing leather jackets as well, so it had to be a funny sight. We were making good money, though, making a couple of thousand per gig.

After Silver City, we were in Los Cruces, New Mexico before our next gig in Lubbock, Texas.

So, the drummer and I decided were going to go into Juarez, Mexico to buy some more leather and party. We park on the US side, walk across the border, and were doing some shopping and whatnot. We run into this American guy who said he was AWOL from the military. We were hanging out with him and he says he knows where we can get some hot Mexican teenage girls. It was always rumored—Mexico and hot teenage prostitutes—so we were interested to see what it was all about.

He takes us into this little bar and says, "Sit down, have a few drinks, and I'll set the whole thing up for you." We sit at the bar, and the bartender says tequila shots are five for a quarter. I say, "Okay, give us a quarter's worth." That became a few more quarters worth, and before you know it, we are woo-hoo, feeling no pain.

By now, we are hungry and this old lady walks in, selling four tacos for a buck. Pretty soon, the AWOL guy comes back in, and says, "You didn't buy tacos, did you?" We knew that wasn't good, and then he told us the old lady made the tacos from rat meat.

So the AWOL guy sends us upstairs, and says, "The mamacita will see you now." We

head upstairs, and sure enough, there is this old lady who tells us to drop our pants so she can check for disease. We drop our drawers, and two young Mexican kids run in and take our wallets and run. We start swinging at anything that moves and are chasing these Mexican kids through these alleys of Juarez, and we have no clue where in the hell we are.

We finally find a taxicab, and after threatening the driver for about 10 minutes or so, actually get him to drive us to the border. We get to the border and the border guard asks for our IDs. We have to tell the whole story and finally are able to get back over into the States and back to our room.

We get back to our hotel and we lay down after this whole ordeal, only to get dysentery from the rat tacos and find ourselves running to the bathroom every ten minutes. The dysentery lasted a month, and there were times it would hit us while we were on stage and had to drop our instruments or drum sticks and run for the head.

So, during that tour, we were almost killed, tried in a kangaroo court in New Mexico, got our wallets stolen, and got dysentery, all in the span of a couple of weeks before we even continued the tour into Lubbock.

SC: After all that, the show must go on, as they say, and you were still hitting the road to play the Lubbock show?

GS: Yeah. We were all excited, though, as we heard all of these stories about the girls in Texas. The one thing we were scared about was that in those days, if you were caught with pot, it was a life sentence. We get to the hotel in Lubbock, unhook the trailer and everything, and decided to go get some beer. We would carry our pot in these little film cans and hide them around various places of the Cadillac.

So, we're driving to get some beer, and we get pulled over. The cop asks, "Can I see your license?" and, once again, I have to tell him the story about Juarez, but he does not want to hear it. I hadn't been able to deposit the money from our last couple of gigs, so I have no ID, a bag of money with five thousand dollars in it, and some pot as I'm talking to this cop who doesn't want to hear anything from these longhaired hippies. So, he arrests us, they confiscate the car, and tell us they are going to search every inch of the Caddie. I'm in jail again, only a few days after the last time I was in jail in New Mexico, making another call to the lawyer to try and get some ID.

Fortunately, our attorney was able to telex our ID's, and the show promoter contacted the police and got them to release us without finding the pot. We got back to the hotel and the first thing we did was smoke all of the pot to try and destroy the evidence.

SC: I have to ask, back then, was pot all dirt weed?

GS: Yeah, the majority was Mexican dirt weed, loaded with seeds, but every once in a while, you could get Acapulco Gold, which was far better. I think it was $15 bucks an ounce for Acapulco Gold. Panama Red was another one of the premium types of pot you could get for that price, but generally, it was always dirt weed loaded with seeds. Every now and then, though, you could get a hold of some good stuff.

SC: So, you smoke all of your pot and then the tour continues?

GS: Yeah, it continued. That was back in '66-'67, so we kept playing after that.

Below (left to right)
* The Beat.... - I mean the Jerms
A cover of THE NOTE's predecessor, *King Harvest Review*, which was edited by NOTE staff writer Robert C. Wilson, aka Ranger Bob Wilson
Photos by George Olson, "House Photographer" for Mid-Continental Prod. in the mid-sixties

The original members of The Jerms, Tom Jacoby keyboards, Larry Burton guitar, Galen Senogles bass, and Mike Doyle drums live on stage in 1965.

I remember in Lubbock, after the show, we met two of the most beautiful girls we had ever met. We brought them back to the hotel room and got them in bed when the phone rings. I answer it, and it's this booming male voice that says, "I'm her boyfriend. I'm in the parking lot. The girls are underage, and I've got a .357 magnum that I will come in and shoot up the place with it if you don't send the girls out." You learn a lot when you are on the road...in that case, I learned a lot in two or three weeks. I learned never to bring pot to Texas, and to leave the teenage girls alone. The girls were awfully cute, so that was tough.

Later, we were designated a "traveling circus."

SC: Is that what you called yourself?

GS: No, that is what we were called by some small-town sheriff. We were playing Rapid City, South Dakota and driving to Billings, Montana or Cody, Wyoming. It was outside one of the national parks, and this gig was in an auditorium where we had arranged a 70/30 split with the promoter, where we got 70% of the gate, and the promoter got 30%.

So, we are in the auditorium and there is no one in there—and I mean no one. The promoter says, "Start to play and they will come in." We are playing for 30 minutes and see people dancing out on the street outside and still not a soul has paid. So I stop the show and pretty soon, once again, here comes the sheriff.

Sheriff says, "You have to play." I am arguing with the sheriff, and we pack all of our equipment and get ready to leave when, once again, we get arrested. We get taken into the jailhouse, and the sheriff is thumbing through this big book, trying to find something to charge us with, and finally comes up with some rule about "traveling circuses" where we needed to pay a fee. So, I simply paid the fee and they let us go. That was rock and roll in The Sixties.

SC: This was still '66-'67, right?

GS: Right.

SC: During this time, your band was harassed because of their appearance. Did you have any security concerns?

GS: Of course! I was always concerned for our survival, but we had to learn ways of protecting ourselves.

One of the ways I learned very early on—I can give you an example I remember well...

We were playing a small college-town in the Midwest, at a beer joint where all the college students would hang out. On this night, this one guy came up and stood right in front of me while we were performing our set and kept shouting profanities and anything else to degrade me and threatened that, "When you get off of this stage, I'm going to beat the shit out of you."

He was a big guy, (I figured he was on the football team). When we were about to finish the last song of the set, I began making the announcement that we were going to take a 15-minute break. So, I unplugged the cord on my Fender Stratocaster to the amp, then unhooked my guitar strap from the bottom with my right hand, and let the guitar slide down to the stage floor. While I continued talking, I grabbed it with two hands and proceeded to swing it like a bat whacking him in the head, knocked him out, and he landed halfway across the dance floor. The crowd started cheering and the bouncer and the owner picked him up and carried him out on the street.

I thought we were going to get thrown out, but instead the owner came back to me and said, "Good job, but make sure you don't take more than a 15-minute break." This happened to me more than once.

Another time, we were taking Interstate 80 from Omaha to South Dakota or something. It was a full-blown blizzard, and some of the people in town told us not to go because of the weather, but for some reason, we decided to go ahead and leave.

We were about 20 miles out of town, driving in some of the worst blizzard conditions I had ever seen. As we kept driving, the road became a one-lane road. We were driving behind this big rig, using its tire tracks as our trail to ride behind, in this big school bus that was The Jerms' touring bus at the time.

Willie Leacox driving The Jerms bus into the ditch before becoming drummer for America.

I decided to let our drummer Willie Leacox drive, and I have a story about him. He ended up getting an audition to be the drummer for America, and actually won the job and, I think, is still their drummer today. I got to hang out with them at the Caribou Ranch out in Colorado, and they actually got to work with George Martin as he produced some of their albums. Willie was a good drummer.

So, anyways, even though I drove most of the time, this time I let him drive. I told him, "Just follow the semi," but he couldn't resist trying to pass. He said, "It's going too damn slow and I am passing it," and the next thing I knew, we were off the road and in a ditch we couldn't get out of, and it's during the storm of the century.

The snow is coming down, and we only had this little teeny heater that ran off the engine. As the heater ran, we could see the gas gauge going down. So, we decided that we had to do something, because at that point, we all felt it was a real possibility that we were going to die in the storm.

We had passed a rest stop a few miles back, and we decided to flip a coin to see who would walk to the rest stop and call for help. Willie Leacox and I lost the draw, so we put on all of our clothes to walk to this rest area. By the time we got there, my legs were frozen, and we were both shivering and numb from the cold. We found the payphone, and we called the Omaha police, telling them we need help.

The dispatcher at the other end of the line said, "You need help? Get in line. Besides, do you think we want to die in the snow to rescue you?" and then click—they hung up on us. We called for help, and they hung up on us.

So, we had to walk back to the bus. All four of us got in one bunk, and did whatever we could to stay warm. The next day, I stood on the road and tried to flag down a truck to help pull us from the ditch, and no one was stopping at all. Finally, I took my moneybag and a handful of money, started waving it around, and sure enough, the first rig that sees me stopped.

The driver said, "I am not supposed to help you and can get in trouble, but how much money is that?" I told him it was $400 bucks, and that was enough to get him to help us. We got back on the road and to the next town.

I was never as so happy to see a city in my life. We went into this little diner for some coffee and food, and it was literally the happiest I had ever been, sitting inside a little diner in a small town. I think I might have gone home with the waitress, if memory serves, so it was really the highs and lows of being a traveling band in the 60s in the Midwest.

SC: While you were stuck in that ditch in the Midwest, during that blizzard, you must have been thinking and having flashbacks about the near miss with Columbia Records, and what could have been. Simon and Garfunkel were topping the charts, and you were stuck in a ditch during storm of the century.

GS: I don't know what I was thinking about, other than survival at that time. But, now that you put it that way, it probably had to have crossed my mind at some point.

"Damn I miss this guitar! I don't remember what happened to it but I can tell you it was not the guitar that was stolen by Snoop Dog and his thieving posse, they stole my white Stratocaster while I was working with El DeBarge " -Galen Senogles

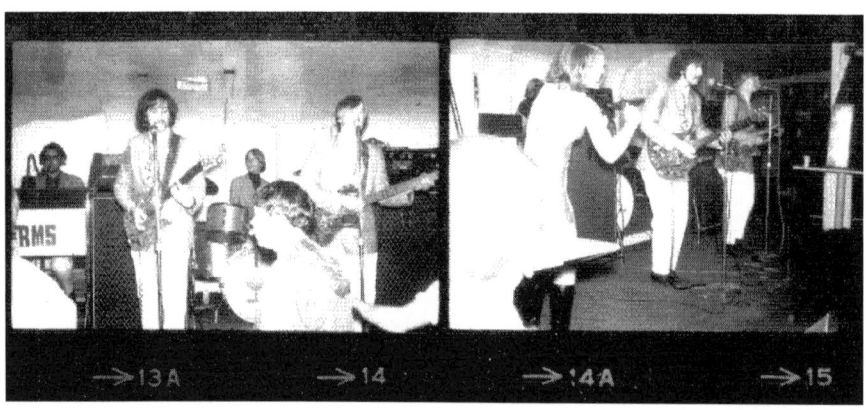

34

Not too long after that our fame grew a bit and we started playing with bigger, more established headline acts like Steppenwolf and Jefferson Airplane, though, stuff like that became less and less of a concern. I figured that they weren't going to let anything happen to Grace Slick, so playing on the same bill with her and other big acts meant those issues kind of went away and didn't happen as often.

SC: So, you opened for Steppenwolf, but they weren't really as popular as they were in the early 70s, then, right?

GS: Yeah. I can't remember the exact date, but by '67 and '68, we were opening for some really big names. Black Sabbath, Mountain, Jefferson Airplane, Three Dog Night, and all of those acts.

SC: Any stories about Black Sabbath and Ozzy?

GS: I am sure I must have partied with Ozzy at some point during those shows but there are none specifically that comes to mind. The stories about Ozzy with the drink and the drugs really became far more common in the late 70s. The stories I can still remember came from Three Dog Night. We really got along with them and they invited me back to their room. Chuck (Negron) was a really cool guy. There was another guy in the band, who they say went nuts, but Chuck was always cool. Steppenwolf were cool guys as well.

At that time, though, the audiences were changing, with more people taking acid and other drugs. It was hard to get a reaction, and the people in the front row would say stuff like, "You're dripping, man." You just couldn't even talk to them they were so whacked out.

SC: So, when you started, it was more like the screaming girls, but at this point, it was more heavy and drug-fueled?

GS: Exactly. When we started, it felt like The Beatles with the girls and the screams, but then it was all that West Coast stuff happening with The Doors and that type of thing. Then, Woodstock hit, and everything changed.

All of these promoters thought they were going to be able to produce Woodstock 2, and it wasn't just doing an auditorium, it was all of these festivals with all of these bands that promoters thought they could take an obscure cornfield in Iowa and somehow make it into a magical event. It was a nightmare.

SC: How so?

GS: You would be playing in the middle of this cornfield, and it would start pouring down rain. You would be stuck in a huge mud puddle for three or four days with people shitting all over each other, and just horrible conditions. It really got messy and ugly, and overall just a very bad experience for everyone involved.

SC: It wasn't like now, where they would have porta-potties, hand sinks, and stuff like that?

GS: No, these promoters weren't prepared at all. They just booked a huge area and chased the money. They never thought about food, drinks, sanitation, or any of that. If there was a road in and a road out, that was pretty much good enough for some promoter to try and make money out of it.

There were some good shows...We played with Sly and the Family Stone and some others. A lot of the times though it would turn into a nightmare for one reason or another.

SC: Any others you remember?

GS: I probably played with just about everybody at one time or another. It was about this time with the promoters and the whole scene—I think—where I started burning out on doing the whole music thing. I kept track of all my mileage that I drove and we went from the Cadillac to buying this bus, and I was good about recording all of the mileage.

SC: By this time, it's 1969, and you are getting cheated and bamboozled with crappy tours and screwed, right?

GS: Yeah, for sure. You were getting screwed and cheated with a lot more frequency. The record companies screwed me more than anybody, but I'll get into that later. I have no sympathy for them with digital copies, pirating, file swapping, and all of that—they deserve everything they get.

I still get some royalties, but probably pennies to what I should be getting.

SC: We will get into that later for sure, but one quick question on that subject: do you get royalties for your engineering work on Pink Floyd's *The Wall*?

GS: No, I only get royalties for the albums where I acted as producer. Being that I only produced a few where I got credit…if you were a writer, a producer, or the publisher, you would get royalties. If you were in the band, then see you later. A few of the bigger acts get paid, but the record companies basically pay that to ensure the next record. If the record companies don't think the next record will sell, they don't pay and it's see you later.

SC: So you were tired of the whole scene? How so?

GS: Everything just got bigger and bigger and bigger. We went from the Cadillac to this school bus I bought and had customized. We were also paying roadies and staff, and spending money on fancy cars, and the evolution from the little band in the Midwest to playing these tours was just getting bigger, bigger, and bigger.

I mentioned how I recorded the mileage…

I sat down and looked at all of the mileage I had driven across the US, and figured out that I had driven to the moon and back and was actually half way back to the moon again. So, I had to ask myself, "Do I want to keep driving?"

The Midwest is a whole lot of driving. It is so spread out, and I realized I wasn't making the money doing one-nighters, and it wasn't as fun as it once was. From there, I decided to start playing the clubs were I could stay and play for a couple of weeks and not have to drive all over. So, I started playing clubs in Denver, Houston, Atlanta, and Oklahoma.

SC: Was the whole band still playing with you, and were you still called The Jerms?

GS: Yeah, nothing had changed really at all. I was still the leader, and we were still doing some originals and covers.

It was the early 70's and we were playing a club in Chicago. That's where I got into hockey as well at the old Chicago Stadium. I got into a club called Rush Up. It was by the Sears Tower on Rush Street. The club owner was a guy named Don Lolly. It was the place where Chaka Khan and Chicago got their starts. It was a big deal, but they made you play from 9pm to 4am each night—that was the kind of place it was. It was Chicago, and man, did I learn about Chicago!

SC: How so?

GS: Well, the first thing I remember was Don Lolly asking if everyone in the band was over 21. I said the drummer wasn't 21, so he asked what his name was, and told us to come back in two hours. We come back in two hours, and he got a motorcycle license and a bunch of other receipts and documents to show that he is over 21. He [Don Lolly] hands us all of this stuff and says, "If anyone asks, he is now over 21."

SC: So, that was your first taste of the Chicago music scene?

GS: It was the first of many experiences. The next thing I learned was that the promoter came in on the first night to collect money from the owner. He owed us six thousand dollars and it was 4am. I go to the bar to get my money and there are two cops there at the bar. The first thing he does is pay off the two cops, and then he gives me my money. He then introduced me to the cops, and said, "Don't worry, they will take care of you."

SC: So this was very different from the cops in Texas and in New Mexico, then, because these cops in Chicago were on the payroll?

GS: Yeah, it was the first time I had ever met a cop that was on my side, and whom I didn't think was going to harass me. Call it corruption, but was I ever glad to know a couple of cops who weren't going to automatically take me into the station! After the cops got their money and left, Don told me, "Don't embarrass the cops if you get into any trouble. Put a fifty-dollar bill in their hand with your driver's license. Don't embarrass them with a twenty." A month later, I get pulled over on the Eisenhower Freeway and I'm scared because I am actually bribing a cop with the fifty-dollar bill trick. He took the money and let me go.

SC: Fifty was the magic number for a Chicago cop in the early 70s?

GS: It was one of many lessons.

We also had two vans, and learned that Chicago is a city that doesn't have a lot of parking spots. After two months, we probably had a thousand parking tickets. I remember our keyboard player wallpapering his room with them, so there were tons. We were doing some other dates in Illinois when I got a call from Don Lolly, who said he wanted us back at Rush Up. I told him there was only one problem: that of the parking tickets.

So, Don charged me a hundred bucks to talk to his attorney about the tickets, and sure enough, his attorney took care of each and every ticket. I really liked Chicago!

SC: Say what you will about the law, but that's certainly easier, right?

GS: Yeah, I loved that part of playing Chicago. It was far easier doing business in Chicago than it was in Kansas.

SC: What happened in Kansas?

GS: Well, between the gap of all the pop festivals and club dates, I was back in Kansas doing some local dates and whatnot. We were coming back from a show in Liberal, Kansas in a city called Salina, Kansas, and once again, we had a little pot.

By this time, I knew more about pot laws, and told all of the guys in the band that if we got pulled over to keep the pot in their pockets, because they couldn't search without a reason. It was two or three in the morning, and we pull into a Holiday Inn to get some breakfast.

As we leave, the police had the whole area road-blocked. They pull us from the car and it was 20 degrees outside, so we're shivering and it's cold. Our drummer got scared and threw his pot under the driver's seat. I had mine in my pocket, but for whatever reason, he panicked. All of a sudden, one of the cops says, "We found your Marijuana," and the cop standing next to me cocks his shotgun and is pointing the barrel six inches from my face.

So we are outside in Podunk, Kansas at 4 or 5 in the morning in 20 degree weather about to be arrested for pot, when another car pulls in with a bunch of guys in suits. The others there were small-town cops. As the regular cops were talking to the guys in suits, I had time to toss my pot into a ditch somewhere. After a meeting between the regular cops and the suits, one of the guys in a suit comes over and asks if I'm the leader, and tells me he is with the KBI (the Kansas Bureau of Investigation), and actually says, "Nice to meet you."

He goes on to say they were looking for robbery suspects, and even though they found our marijuana, they did not have the right to search the car, so we were free to go. Then the local cop comes back and starts yelling at us to never set foot in town again as we are driving out.

SC: Another close call for you and the band. How many others were there?

GS: We probably had the scariest moment I ever had back in Chicago.

We were still at the Rush Up, and I had a band rule. I insisted that, when it came to girls and parties, you always brought them to the hotel and never go back to their homes, because you never knew what you were walking into. You take them back to the hotel, and its relatively safe. You go to their place, and it could be walking into an angry boyfriend with a gun ready to blow your head off.

SC: That makes sense.

GS: Well, that was our golden rule, and I was the first to break it. There was a gal who would stay until the club closed a few weeks in a row who was gorgeous. I actually thought I was in love. We would stay at the bar and talk, and after a couple of weeks, she invited me back to her place. So, we get into her Volkswagen, driving to the north side of town, and I am looking at her and just thinking this was the greatest night of my life.

We go inside her apartment building and take the elevator up the second floor to get to her room. She asks if I want to smoke a joint. Ten seconds later, her phone rings and I hear her saying, "I told you it was over…No…Stop calling me—it's over!" and that sort of thing. She looks at me and says, "We have to get out of here now. That was my ex and he saw you come in with me."

So we get into the elevator, and as the elevator door opens, this guy is holding a .357 with his left hand and pointing it between my eyes. With his right hand, he punched the girl in the nose and breaks it, with blood splattering everywhere. I've got blood splattered all over me, and I'm feeling like a pansy standing next to this gorgeous girl bleeding profusely from her broken nose and staring down the barrel of some angry ex-boyfriend's gun. He looks at me and simply says, "Run, motherfucker."

I ran like I never ran before—until I was out of breath and in some part of the city I didn't know. I finally found a pay phone and called the hotel to have someone pick me up and take me back. Will never forget that night.

SC: Just one of many lessons from life on the road, eh?

GS: It was almost the final lesson on the road. At least the guy was cool enough to let me go. I was still shocked she set me up as well as she did. Blood was spattered everywhere…I will never forget. After that, I started carrying a knife.

SC: Was that incident indirectly or directly responsible for you getting out of the music business as a performer?

GS: Yes, that was right at the end when I decided I was done. I already wanted to try and get to LA, because it was the scene at the time, and that incident was pretty much pivotal for me to pack my stuff and move.

SC: Had you already played some clubs in Los Angeles, and were you familiar with it?

GS: Yeah, we played some shows in LA, but they were at really crappy clubs off Lankershim Blvd. and those areas. They only wanted cover tunes, and we always felt like we were simply a jukebox, as opposed to musicians playing our own songs. The group Kansas made it after getting spotted by a producer who happened to stumble into the bar they were playing at. It was just the luck of the draw for them.

I never forgot what may have been, had we taken Bob Johnston's deal offered to us by Columbia way back when, and how things may have been different. Heck, had that been the case, we probably wouldn't be sitting and talking at all right now. For Kansas, they got spotted, got a contract offer, said, "Let's do it," and the rest was history for them.

I can't tell you how many times we were starving at 3 or 4 in the morning in some Midwest town, and weren't even able to get served because of our look. Again, I was always hearing the "Is he a boy or a girl?" routine and it was almost comical in that it never changed or varied. After a while, it was like these guys were reading from the same script because it was always the same lines and routine. The state and the face may have been different, but the lines never changed. There were some real redneck areas out there, where the locals always wanted to cut your hair, or beat you up, or shoot you, or whatever.

In my opinion, if you had a good act, you had a pretty good shot at making it if you lived on the East Coast or the West Coast. If you were from the Midwest, you were in the middle of nowhere, and the record companies had no reason at all to go to Kansas, Nebraska, or wherever when the LA, New York, and San Francisco scenes were filled with some talented groups. We had one or two shots—we just didn't make it.

SC: So, after all of these tours and crazy experiences, when did you finally move out to LA?

GS: That was probably 1971.

SC: Did you have any idea that you were going to be an engineer or producer and still be in the music business? What were your plans?

GS: I was always the sound guy for the band, so I knew I wanted to be an engineer. I was always into tweaking the dials and making sure we sounded good. I was always on the cutting-edge. I was one of the first to play a Danelectro guitar, and I was the first guy to order a Marshall amp in the United States.

I had one of the first Marshall amps ever imported. I was one of the first guys to play a Fuzz Tone, and at one time, I built the unit directly into my guitar. We would go through small towns, and I would always check out the pawn shops and music shops for deals.

SC: Do you realize what that would be worth today?

GS: That's nothing. I bought an old Fender Strat from a pawn shop that only had three serial numbers.

When I moved out to LA, I was broke and sold it for $400 dollars. Last I heard, they are now worth $15,000 or something. When I was recording with Pink Floyd, David Gilmour had an amazing guitar collection he was using during the sessions. Had I saved every guitar, amp, or effect I used, I would be rich.

SC: I really look forward to talking about your stories from the 70s. How did you break into being an engineer?

GS: That's a good question. There was a little studio off of Pico Blvd. called TPC, and the owner's name was Joe Klein. We paid them to cut records for The Jerms. When I came back to LA, I had nothing and I remembered their names and that studio specifically for whatever reason.

For some reason, I decided to marry some groupie from Kansas and take her with me to LA. Anyhow, I remembered a few of the guys from the studio, so one of the first things I did when I got into LA was hit the studio and try and get a job. They said they weren't hiring and didn't need anybody, so I started volunteering to clean the studio and just started showing up every day. Finally, someone called in sick or something, and they asked me if I could work on a session. This was back when most were still using eight-tracks, and this studio was a 12-track studio, so it was cutting-edge for the time. There were a lot of demo's being cut there, and I can tell you a great story if you want to hear it.

SC: Of course!

GS: I was the guy who cut and engineered Billy Joel's "Piano Man" demo.

SC: No kidding?

GS: He came in with Artie Ripp—who we used to call "Artie Ripoff"—who was Billy's manager at the time. He came in and I recorded that demo with just Billy doing vocals while playing the piano.

SC: So, you are telling me the first time Billy Joel cut the demo for "Piano Man," you were there in the studio?

GS: Yeah, I was the one who did the sound, the mix, everything on the demo. I was at the board. When Joel signed with Columbia, they couldn't recreate the piano and the vocal sounds they got on the demo. They tried everything to get the sound and couldn't do it. So, they decided the demo was the best take. After that, they simply added the rest of the production for "Piano Man" around that same demo that I actually recorded.

The thing was, he was so goddamn good that you didn't need to do anything else to improve it.

I was also there with Clive Davis when he started Arista Records. I was there with Carly Simon and James Taylor when they recorded "Mockingbird." I've got enough stories about Ringo and Jim Keltner alone to write a book.

*****

SC: When we left off, you were telling us the story about recording the demo for Billy Joel's *Piano Man.*

GS: Ah yes, Artie Ripp! He later opened his own studio and had some successful artists…some girl artist who had some hits…

The studio was located off of Whitsett and Moorpark in Studio City, I believe. What would happen at that time was I would be the house band, where I would play guitar and had some of my friends from Kansas—the state as opposed to the band—to be backup musicians. If a musician came in and didn't have a band, we would write down the chords and act as studio musicians and the house band, and they would pay us $500 bucks.

SC: And this was still the first little studio in LA on Pico Blvd.?

GS: Yeah, this all took place in the demo studio. Most of the work we did was like Billy Joel, with one guy and a piano, and if they wanted a backup band, I hired my buddies.

One time, this guy named Tommy McReynolds came in. He had a hit with the song *"It Never Rains in California,"* which we had recorded for him. He came in, and I think he was with Columbia or CBS at the time, and they wanted more songs.

So, he came in, wanting the house band and I to record some more songs for him and his record deal. Since we had this little crappy demo studio, he asked us to go to another location to record the masters, and that was the first time I was able to work in the Producer's Workshop. We worked as musicians for a three-song deal, and I played live with him a couple of times, but after that, he worked with studio guys.

When I got into the Producer's Workshop, I was just awestruck with the equipment and being able to work in a real, full-fledged production studio. "Oh my God, a real studio!"

SC: Was that 24-track back then?

GS: At that time, it was still 16-track. When I looked at the control board and equipment, I knew I had to work there. So, I went over after the session was over and started talking with some of the staff, and said, "Hey, the trash is full and the bathroom is kind of dirty." The staff there said they didn't have the budget to hire a cleaning staff, so I just asked if I could do it. So, when I wasn't working at the demo studio, I was spending all my free time at the Producer's Workshop cleaning and hanging out again and again.

SC: That was the same trick you used to get into the demo studio as well, right?

GS: Yeah, and as I got to know the people and spend more time there, I met a genius electronic guy named Bud Wyatt. He built the place all by hand. Producer's Workshop was originally Continental Sound, and was owned by Liberace. It was owned and run by AVI Records Entertainment, which was the name of his company.

SC: So that was how you ended up meeting Liberace?

GS: Yeah. We can talk about that later, but Liberace was a great guy.

Anyhow, there are your genius musicians, and then there are your genius electronic guys. Bud Wyatt was a genius electronic guy. Those guys are hard to talk to because they are out there in another zone, but he was easy to relate with and he liked me as a musician. So, I started picking his brain and learning the board and getting some tips from him. I was doing that for about three months.

One day, I walked in and they asked if I was ready. In those days, they had a producer, a first engineer, and a second engineer. The second engineer was the guy who knew the studio, the setup, and the room; and who took directions from the first engineer, who was working with the producer. The second engineer was generally one of the better-known guys who recorded in a lot of different studios, so he didn't have the knowledge of specific rooms.

So, the second engineer was the guy who knew all of the nuances, and the in's and out's of that specific room. Anyhow, one day some guy called in and missed a session and they asked me to sit in as the second engineer. Of course, you're never going to say no, so that's how I got the job at Producer's Workshop, and got to work with John Lennon on Ringo's album and all that.

Luckily, the guy who called in never came back.

SC: What year was this?

GS: This was probably 1971 or 1972. I did some early stuff with Bachman, Turner, Overdrive, and Alice Cooper. We also did work with Alice Cooper's guitarist, Dick Wagner, who got a recording deal. We were also doing some stuff for Shelter Records—*Up on the Tight Rope* with Leon Russell I can remember clearly. Russell had a lot of hits back in those days, and I worked closely with his producer, Denny Cordell.

What was good about these recordings was that it allowed me to get enough work under my belt and work long enough that I got to do some work as the first engineer. One of the first groups I worked with was a band from Gainesville, Florida called "Mudcrutch."

SC: Really? So you cut Tom Petty's first demo when he came out to LA?

GS: Yeah. Tom and Benmont Tench...I was the guy who recorded their first demos and then their entire first album. I had the original tapes for years and tried to get them back to Tom, but could never get through his management to give him the tapes back. They (the tapes) literally sat in my closet and garage for years. I am still always amazed his management not only weren't interested in the tapes, but didn't even pass along the message to Tom himself.

SC: Do you still have them?

GS: No. At one point, after his management expressed no interest in them, I had thought about pirating them and putting them out as a bootleg or something, but I'm not that kind of guy, and that wasn't something I was going to do. I told them I am going to throw them away and they just never got back with me, so I did just that.

SC: When was this?

GS: That was probably the late 80s or something. That was about the time a lot of those old tapes were converted into digital and all that. Those were the quarter-inch tapes in these big boxes that I'm carrying around. I think I actually just threw them in the garbage or something.

I remember as well in the early 70s doing more stuff with Shelter Records. We did Phoebe Snow's *Poetry Man*. I recorded a big upright bass on that track. About that time as well I started with Clive Davis. He had just started Arista Records, and what happened was that all of that work was done for Columbia, with Bill Schnee, Richard Perry with Ringo, Carly Simon, and all that stuff. Davis and all of those guys were padding the bills.

SC: Okay, to recap, you pretty much solidified your position as 2nd engineer at the Producer's Workshop, and did a good enough job that you routinely worked with the biggest acts of the day.

GS: That is pretty much it. The work I did with Mudcrutch was my first gig as first engineer and working with Denny Cordell. What Denny did as producer—and he was a good producer—was record all of these songs and he would listen to them, come back in, and have a meeting with Tom [Petty] and say, "I don't think your drummer is good enough," so they would lose the drummer.

SC: So that was it and they fired the drummer?

GS: That was one of the first ones. Next, it was, "I don't think your bass player is good enough."

In the meantime, we didn't record everything there. Tom really liked working with me, so we also recorded at this studio off of Santa Monica Blvd. called "The Village Recorder." That was my first independent job and I was very happy, seeing as I got paid and got to be the big shot in the studio.

Anyway, basically what Denny was doing was eliminating everyone in the band until it was just Tom and Benmont. They were the talent.

SC: So, let me ask you: being there, was it obvious the other guys weren't as good or talented as Petty and Benmont?

GS: Yeah. Each time Denny made a move, it improved the band, and it was all about Tom, because he was the obvious star. They never put any of that stuff out, which was surprising because it was good.

SC: Were any of the songs on the demo songs that later became hits? Was "American Girl" or "Refugee" or one of those hits part of the demo?

GS: There were some that ended up on his first album, but I can't recall the exact song. Once again, it was good stuff, and in the late 80s, I really was hoping it could get released because I had the tapes. When I called Petty's management, I just asked them, "Do you know what you've got here? Tom Petty raw? I mean, you don't want it? Fine."

SC: So Tom liked working with you. What happened?

GS: At that time, they started losing their budget to record. Tom took me out to Leon Russell's house because he had put a studio there.

SC: Was that in the Hollywood Hills?

GS: I think it was Encino—somewhere in The Valley. I was still new to LA at that time, so I still really didn't know my way around.

SC: Leon Russell was huge back then, right? In the early 70s, was Leon Russell as big as Dylan?

GS: Oh yeah, he was big! He made a ton of great songs, a ton of money, and was one of the major draws to Shelter Records.

SC: It is funny now that Leon Russell is considered some B-rate act or footnote in history, because in the 70s, he was a god.

GS: Like I said, he was selling a ton of his own records and writing big time hits for other artists. I went out to his home and at that time, I was working for free because Tom had made me the promise that, when he made it, he would remember me and all of that stuff.

It was mind-boggling to be working at Russell's studio as an engineer, because they had a piano in the downstairs closet and the mics all over the place. I finally told Tom, "I love you, man, but can't keep hanging." At that time, I was still working in the other studio, and getting better jobs and working with Ringo. I look back now, and think, "Man! If only I could have hung in there!" but that was the business, and in life, you make choices.

SC: That is true in any business, and true in life for that matter.

GS: So, I was working with Phoebe Snow and that was when I really got to know Clive Davis. Clive was really smart. What he would do was hire all of these songwriters, like Randy Edelman, Melissa

Manchester, and those sorts and give them record deals. He would get them into the studio to record their albums, and then would take their best songs, and give it to Barry Manilow. Then, Barry Manilow would have a huge hit with one of their songs.

SC: So he would basically use the lure of cutting a record to take their best songs for one of his established acts?

GS: Yes. That is how he would get the songs. It was pretty smart, so by signing them as music acts and not songwriters, he was able to get more money from licensing and publishing and all of that.

Clive was a smart man. He had a good ear, too. He would come down at the start, so I met him a few times. I would be a fly on the wall while these angry artists would give him hell. Melissa Manchester in particular was irate at Clive, as she wanted to be an artist, and Clive would just use her to get songs. That was a whole crazy phase I went through.

At that point, I was still on the janitor's salary—believe it or not—so I was trying to get a raise. Even though I'm working as a first engineer with these huge names, they still had me on the janitor's salary. AVI Records (who owned the place), Seymore Heller, Ed Cobb, and these other guys wouldn't work with me on my salary, so I started sending my resume out.

One day, I get a call from Elektra Records—probably around 1973 would be my guess. Bruce Morgan calls and says, "I like your resume and want to interview you." So, I go down and he goes into this big story about how they are going to build this million dollar, state-of-the-art studio, and they wanted me to help build it and be the main engineer with a, "You built it, you know it" type of deal. I got on board and it was like three months to build the whole thing.

Right when we were finishing, we get the word that Elektra had merged with another label called Asylum that was run by this new kid named David Geffen. So, Bruce comes in and says, "I guess we will all be good as they've got a ton of artists and an A&R staff who wants to sign some new acts."

I ended up being the guy who cut the demos for Jackson Brown, The Eagles, and Linda Rondstadt. The way they did it back then—and I'm in there when this is coming down, and this is why those groups were successful—they would bring in the band to record six or seven songs and then send it up to A&R, who would listen for a week and come back with, "We like Jackson Brown," or "We like so-and-so," and based on that, we would record more songs. So, Jackson would come back in, and we would cut another four or five songs.

SC: Yeah, I know at that time there was a lot of musicians living off Laurel Canyon who were hanging and writing together. The Eagles, Jackson Brown, Warren Zevon…

GS: That's right. I still live off Laurel Canyon, and when I finally got my own studio, that was where it was located. I think I have a whole early catalog of Asylum promo records still in the shrink-wrap. I know I still have this rock from some Linda Ronstadt promo.

SC: What was Linda Ronstadt's deal?

GS: She was making her way to the top by sleeping with everybody, or at least that was the hot rumor, but she was nice. She would come around wiggling her ass to everybody and running around. Every A&R guy knew she was laying everybody, and at one time, I think she had her eye on David [Geffen]. Anyhow, based on that, we knew she was going to have a promising career.

SC: Tell me more about the studio.

GS: It was Studio A, and it was a state-of-the-art, million-dollar studio—floating floors and the whole bit. They wanted us to try and record [quadraphonic], but me and Bruce both knew it wasn't going to happen. Six months later or thereabouts, we got the word that David Geffen himself was going to come in.

I was working with Bread—actually it was just David Gates—as he was recording a solo album. So, Geffen walks in, and it was he, David Gates, Bruce, myself, and some other person with Geffen whom I didn't know. Geffen comes in, and when I shook his hand, it was like a wet noodle. He was this little Jewish guy, all hunched over like someone on *The Simpsons* or something.

Anyhow, he takes one look at Studio A, points his finger, and says "Offices," and then walks out. Bruce and I looked at each other, and said "Uh oh," as we knew something wasn't right. About a week later, the word came down that they wanted that area to be offices, so we had to tear everything down and move it into other studios, while our new state-of-the-art studio was converted into offices on the whim of David Geffen.

After that, Bruce came to me and said I was a trooper, his best employee, and blah blah blah…and that he could get me a job in the tape copy room. I helped him move the best equipment into Studio B, which was the room in which The Doors recorded most of their work. The real world of David Geffen was too much for me, as I wanted to be an engineer and not a tape copy guy.

I was helping move the studio when A&R came in and said they had an opportunity for me and wanted to keep me onboard. We get into this car and drive out to Reseda in the Valley, to this house that ended up being the studio where The Monkees recorded.

SC: One of The Monkees?

GS: Mike Nesmith.

I met him and they gave him this studio, as he had signed a deal. The offer was, I could live there for free and record with Nesmith and make the same salary. I said "No way!" All Elektra needed to do is walk in someday and say, "You're gone."

All of those guys were lawyers anyways. They weren't musicians—they were lawyers.

SC: So, was this the point when the music business was becoming more about business and less about music?

GS: Yes and no. They still had music guys making some of the decisions, and one of the things I learned by hanging around the A&R guys was that they would sign an artist to a five-record deal, assume they would have some hits by the fourth or fifth album, and then re-release all of the early work.

SC: Going back to The Eagles; you recorded their early demos? Was that still when Bernie Leadon and Randy Meisner were in the band?

GS: Yeah, I recorded all of those guys' early demo work. My job was to record them and they did it so quick, there was no time to get to know any of those bands. You are looking at a schedule that has all of these band names, and they are all new acts you have never heard of. You took a look at the schedule and saw "The Eagles," and you were like "So what? Who the hell are they?" because then, they were nobodies.

I recorded hundreds of bands.

SC: Was it hard to remember specific things about The Eagles or Jackson Brown because you were working with all these different acts?

GS: Yeah. Basically, I would spend four or five hours—long enough to record a few songs—and then move on to the next band. After I cut the demos, it was up to A&R who, at that point, decided if we brought them back in for more songs.

SC: Back to David Geffen: he comes in, and at the snap of a finger, converts the million dollar studio you helped to build into offices, and at the same time, you lose your gig as engineer, only to be offered a tape room job?

GS: That was it.

I had no idea what I wanted to do, and Bruce was great to help me get unemployment. At that point—because I had some money coming in and had a very strained relationship with my wife—I decided to pack it all up and move back to Kansas.

Back in Kansas, we were living at my dad's house, and my wife was getting uglier by the day, when my dad finally came to me and said, "Son, you've got to get rid of this girl."

Anyhow, I am living in Kansas, and I get this call from the Producer's Workshop, who had no idea I had been laid off and was living in Kansas. They offered to triple my salary and make me studio manager. It wasn't a real hard decision at that point. Had they offered me all of that before coming back to Kansas, I would have never left.

SC: What year was this?

GS: I would think that was late 1973.

SC: As a studio manager, were you working under a producer?

GS: No, as studio manager I was running the place. They wanted me to oversee all of the clients and artist who came in. Some I worked with, some I didn't. A lot of it depended on whom the artist was and what needed to be done.

They gave me the budget to hire a secretary, and we were building a second room. Bud Wyatt came back in and built a mix room along with the recording room. One of the first things I did was hire a friend of mine named Joe Bellamy, who was a keyboard player in my little band. I hired him to do studio work—odds and ends—as I always thought that to work in a studio, you needed to be a musician. If I was going to run a tape machine, I wanted a guy who knew some music.

Anyhow, I was working with Steely Dan on the *Aja* album with Donald Fagen. We were working on *Aja* and still working a 16-track machine—maybe we had converted to the 24-tracks by that time. Standard practice was to set up the tones to a universal setting to normalize the tones and the bias, so they could align the sounds and be in sync if they moved the tapes to another studio.

So, working on *Aja*, Joe Bellamy was working on the album and took a phone call as he was setting the tones, and as he talked on the phone, the tone recording continued while he was involved in this phone call. Long story short, he wiped out the first minute and a half of the song they had recorded the day before. The problem was, it was an intro and a master [recording].

So, here I am, having to tell Donald Fagen that we accidentally erased some of his song and he has to re-record it.

I called Fagan into the office expecting the worse, and told him that if he re-recorded it, I would pay for the session. He came back into my office after they had re-recorded the song and was beaming, saying that he thought the new recording was better than the previous, erased version.

I tell the story not to expose my good friend Joe, but after that, we started recording the tones on the end portion of the tape as opposed to the beginning of the tape. It was later made into company policy not long after, and I hear 20 years later that they still tell that story at recording workshops about this infamous episode in recording history.

SC: So, the Steely Dan erased song is now legendary?

GS: I hear it's the most common and oft-told story for those learning the industry.

SC: Did you get a credit on the *Aja* album for being a producer or involved with the recording?

GS: As the studio manager, I seldom was able to get any credit on albums, as I was busy handling the day-to-day tasks involved in running the studio. Joe got a credit, though; in spite of the fact he erased part of a song with one of the labels biggest bands. My role changed depending on the artist and the level.

At that time, disco was coming around, so we worked a lot with AVI Records, which was owned by Liberace. They were trying to develop disco, so I was running the studio by the day and working with AVI at night. It was a busy time, as I would come into the studio at 11 a.m., and then off to AVI where I'd work until 5 a.m.

SC: What other projects were you working on?

GS: Well, the next thing was Fleetwood Mac with the *Rumours* album. It was after we did the two Ringo albums, and we did both of those Ringo albums with Bill Schnee as the first engineer.

SC: Before we get to Fleetwood Mac, do you want to talk about the work you did with The Beatles?

GS: We were at the Producer's Workshop, and they basically told me to work the machine and do whatever they wanted to do. It was the Ringo album that looked like *Sergeant Pepper*...I think it was *Ringo*. I have the picture of John Lennon and me in the studio somewhere.

Anyhow, John Lennon and George Harrison were there along with Ringo.

The pressure on tape operators is such that you are listening to a song you have never heard, they are throwing things at you left and right, and you are doing individual tracks with no vocals. Being able to punch in and punch out and knowing when to record and when not to record is tough, and when its John Lennon saying, "I want you to get in at the end of the bridge and bring it back to the beginning of the verse," it is even more tough.

You have only heard the song once, and if you don't do it right, or make a couple of mistakes, you are gone.

Anyhow, I was in total awe of John Lennon and we were working together on Ringo's album for about two weeks.

SC: Was he playing guitar or piano?

GS: I remember him mostly playing guitar. We had a house band, and Richard Perry was the producer, but when John came in to record those couple of songs, he was in charge of the studio. And that is saying a lot because Richard Perry *was the man*. There were not too many people in the business who had the power to make Richard Perry take a backseat, but Lennon was and Lennon did. However, John only came in and worked on the songs he wrote for the album and wasn't around at all for the other tracks. He was with May Pang at the time, having broken up with Yoko.

John Lennon at Sunset Sound Studios 1974 with Ringo Star in the back, Richard Perry left, and Galen Senogles right.

SC: Who was in the house band?

GS: If I remember correctly, Nicky Hopkins was playing piano and Klaus Voorman was on bass, with Jim Keltner on drums. I am sure you have heard of Jim Keltner.

SC: Of course! Anyone who calls himself a rock and roll fan knows Jim Keltner. Those two names alone are two legendary figures in the world of rock and roll.

GS: They had the best of everything. The second album I did was *Goodnight, Vienna*. It was at Sunset Sound. Ringo had his drum kit there and he played along, but we turned them off in the studio and had Keltner do all the parts.

Sunset Sound Hollywood Studio 2 where Galen did "Goodnight Vienna" with Ringo and John Lennon in 1974

SC: You mentioned previously that you had a good Jim Keltner story.

GS: After two weeks working with the three Beatles, I am in awe. I am this kid from Kansas working with my idols, and I am trying hard not to make any mistakes and make sure everything is perfect. I am working my butt off, and finally take a 15-minute break. I go outside and stand next to Jim [Keltner] and say something like, "Good job on that song," or something or other. He pulls out a big joint and lights it up and says, "Mary Jane, man," and offers me some. I politely decline, as I am working, wanting to stay sharp, and I am all business.

Anyhow, I ask him how he can play so well after getting high, to which he replied, "I'm on acid and I am trying to come down."

SC: So you are in the studio recording with him, and he is hitting all his marks and being the all-around best drummer in the business, all the while being on acid?

GS: After that, I felt like a lightweight. It blew my mind. I had a whole new respect for Jim Keltner, and he was known for his weird fills, so it kind of made sense after that.

SC: So, you were in the studio watching him play, all impressed, and then later find out he was on acid? Classic! Did the others know he was on acid, or was it a party scene?

GS: I don't think Richard or John knew he was. It was the 70s, though, so drugs and alcohol in the studio weren't uncommon. Looking back, I think John [Lennon] was on speed.

SC: How so?

GS: He would come in and would have rapid-fire discussions with a table full of people at the same time. His brain was going at 110 miles per hour, and he would start a new conversation with someone else while you were mid-sentence, answering a question he specifically asked you. It was amazing—he could carry on five different conversations at the same time.

SC: You really think he was on speed?

GS: Like I said earlier: if he wasn't, his brain was.

I remember we were working six days on, and then Sunday off. I remember going home on Sunday and watching *Yellow Submarine*, which was playing on ABC, and may have been the first run or something.

I go to work on Monday, and—true story—working and about half way through the day, John looked at me and said, "Can't you fucking talk?"

I kind of stuttered, "Uh, er, uh...I saw *Yellow Submarine* last night," at which point he went off on me, saying how he hated the movie, that it cost him millions, ran out of budget to finish it, and that he was mad I even brought it up. If I was quiet before, I certainly wasn't going to pipe up after that.

SC: You had told me how one of your roles was to keep Ringo busy so he would, presumably, not be drinking during the sessions; I understand you played a lot of backgammon with him. What were some other memories of the Ringo sessions, and in particular, George Harrison? What was he like in the studio?

GS: He never spoke—kind of like me after Lennon went off.

SC: Well, he was the quiet Beatle.

GS: Yeah, never said a word. He would come in and I remember him being pretty tall. He would come in with his guitar, head down, and when it was his turn to play, he would play the shit out of his guitar part.

SC: Geoff Emerick, in his book, said that Harrison was, "ham fisted." He said that it took a long time for him to play his solos, that he wasn't that adept as a guitar player, and that it was McCartney who helped him work out most of Harrison's guitar solos. In some ways, Emerick kind of shit on Harrison a bit as a guitar player. Did you see anything while working with him that could confirm or deny that?

GS: My thoughts on that are that I could see that as a possibility in some complicated situations. One of the things John said about every half hour—not kidding—was, "If Paul were here, it would be another fucking definite maybe, ya know?"

So, that gave me some insight into what it must have been like working in the studio with Paul, and here is George, this quiet guy working between Lennon and McCartney. So I could see how, during The Beatles recording, there probably was a lot of pressure on George.

That said, what I saw was that when it was his turn to perform, he played well, but in those sessions, there was no pressure.

I have met Geoff Emerick, and he is a legend, so I can see him coming away with that opinion. However, when I worked with George, he was a professional and had no problems hitting his marks. Working with Ringo was something else though.

SC: Back in those days, Ringo was drinking a lot, right?

GS: Yeah, and he was going through some other things as well. I would see him and ask him how he was doing, and if he was in a bad way. He would say, "I'm just a fucking personality. I can't sing. They just put me up there to be a personality."

On the first album, I didn't notice it [his drinking] as much.

At the Producer's Workshop, it was all business. Over at Sunset Sound and the Record Plant, there were hot tubs and girls and the whole LA scene going on. When I was asked to work on his second album, and I remember I was working on someone else's record at the time, was when they called me to work on *Goodnight, Vienna*.

I think I was the first 2nd engineer ever to be hired as an independent contractor, taking me from another studio to work with Ringo. Working on *Vienna* was when I really got close to Ringo. I worked on the entire album—worked the tape machines, set up the entire room. Bill Schnee really didn't have to do much there, but I was happy to do it, because he taught me everything I knew.

SC: On *Goodnight, Vienna*, you got to know Ringo a bit more than on the *Ringo* album. How did that come about?

GS: Along with running the board and my other various studio tasks, my other assignment was handed down from Richard Perry. That task was to stick with Ringo and do my best to keep him sober so we could record vocals that night. I've got a picture somewhere of Ringo and myself at Sunset Sound.

That was the backgammon era, you could say, because he loved to play.

So, we would sit around in the down time, play backgammon, and talk for a couple of hours. He loved talking about the early days. Even pre-Beatle stories about his days with Rory Storm if memory serves. While we were playing, he would take a bottle of bourbon from his pocket and take a couple of drinks here and there between rolls of the dice.

SC: Did he have a flask, or would he just carry a fifth?

GS: It was a flask, for sure, and once he started drinking, he would get into his, "I'm just a personality, I can't sing" thing that I heard a lot.

SC: Do you think he was afraid to sing?

GS: Yeah, because he didn't think he was any good. I would always try to egg him on with, "I love your songs, and you do a great job."

When it got time to record the vocals, typically, you would set up a mic in the middle of the floor in view of the control room. When it came time to record his vocals, Ringo said, "I can't stand there—you've got to hide me."

They had a thing called a "live booth" that was in the corner of the room, where you cut guide tracks and whatnot. So, he goes into the "live booth," and not only did he record the vocals from there, but he turned his back on us as well. We got it out of him, though, and it was great.

SC: Did he record all of his songs like that on *Goodnight, Vienna*?

GS: Yeah, I think most of the songs were recorded in the live booth. The vocals for "The No No Song" were for sure recorded there. That was a Hoyt Axton song, and I remember a story about that one.

Hoyt Axton came in one day with his guitar and a 45 demo record of the song. So, we sat around and listened to it, and Richard Perry says, "Thank you, Hoyt. I like it."

This will give you an idea of how good of a producer Richard Perry was. Once we heard the demo and Hoyt left—and this was still at the beginning of the album—Richard told Ringo we were going to cut "The No No Song", and Ringo didn't want to do it.

Ringo goes, "I can't sing a fucking song about sleeping on the floor. I'm not going to do it. Forget it. Fuck you!" and he turned around and walked away.

SC: Ringo said that to Richard Perry about "The No No Song"?

GS: Yeah, exact words.

Then, Richard sent me out to go find him. Over the course of the album, Ringo kept saying he wasn't going to do it, and wasn't going to record the song.

Finally, on the last night, at 2 a.m., we are all done recording the last song. Richard says, "One more thing: I want to record this last song," and he got the band to record the music part. The very last thing he managed to do was get Ringo, who was drunk, into the booth to record the vocals, and it ends up becoming the number-one song.

SC: I remember my oldest brother had the 45 of "The No No Song," and I used to listen to it all the time. I could never understand why my parents gave me funny looks every time their six-year-old son was singing about cocaine.

Also, remember the flip side of "Snookeroo?" To this day, "Snookeroo" is still my favorite Ringo song of all time. Elton John wrote it, and Robbie Robertson played guitar. Where you at that recording as well?

GS: Yeah, we didn't have Robbie a lot, but when he was there, he was great to work with. Those sessions were all at Sunset Sound.

SC: Was Elton John there as well?

GS: I don't remember Elton John being there at all during those sessions themselves but he was there for some of the mixing, and it was a long time ago, so it may have been one of those things were Elton recorded his piano part and sent the tapes over to us or something like that.

SC: The beauty of the song is that the piano line is so clearly "Elton John" and the guitar is clearly "Robbie Robertson."

GS: You just shook my memory! We had 2-inch magnetic tape, and Ringo was going back to London to record the piano overdubs. We would put them into these special boxes, but Ringo or someone had forgotten to do it.

The tapes ended up with Ringo, and went through an X-Ray machine at the airport that removed all of the highs. When Elton got back, all the highs were gone and we were all asking, "What the hell happened to our song?" Ringo had this puppy-dog look on his face, thinking he had ruined the tape.

We were lucky, though, because we had kept the safety master and were able to get it back.

SC: What was Robbie like?

SC: Very professional. Robbie would just go to his spot, hit his lines, and really didn't talk at all—just did his job. He was a lot like George Harrison in that aspect.

A good story about Robbie was when I worked on the *Hot Cakes* album, with a pregnant Carly Simon and Richard Perry producing after we did Ringo's album.

That was her album with, "I Haven't Got Time For The Pain," that she wrote about being pregnant. Carly and I got along really well, and she was cool. We had a big Baldwin piano that she played on.

Every morning, I would put some roses and some candy kisses on the piano for her. She loved me for it and it was great. We were working on the album, doing the songs one night, and we had Robbie Robertson, Jim Keltner—Klaus Voorman was there—and some other people…I think Nicky [Hopkins] was there, too.

Carly said that James Taylor was going to come in the studio. So, at 9 at night, James Taylor came in and I could tell he was on heroin. He was all hunched over and gaunt.

Anyhow, he looks at Richard Perry, and said he had an idea that he wanted Carly to remake an old song called, "Mockingbird." Robbie was playing guitar, and they spent a little time rehearsing the parts and the bridge. I am listening to them rehearsing, and my radar is going off that something special is happening, so they say they are going to do a run through, and I hit record.

No one told me to; it was just one of those things I could sense. A minute through, Richard turns and looks at me and says, "Please tell me you got this." They tried 24 more takes of the song, but it was that first run-through that ended up going to number one.

These guys [the musicians] were so good you could feel the magic. Normally, Richard would wear you out, trying to get the best or a better performance, and see if he could get it to the next level. In this case, after one session of "Mockingbird," we got it. It was a fantastic moment. Most of them don't come that easy.

SC: With guys like Robbie and Nicky, you could just see they were the best in the business?

GS: Yeah, they could all do their jobs...

Richard Perry was a controlling producer, and that's what made him good. He would always hire the best musicians and the best of everything. It would be like making a movie and hiring the best writer, the best director, and the best actors. That was Perry, and that's what made him so good. He was demanding, and he would get what he wanted.

In some sessions, Perry would have to stop, and a lot of other musicians would do different things or try something differently, but with Robbie Robertson, he would just nail his lines in one or two takes and it was perfect. You never had to tell Robbie anything, or ever ask him to do anything twice.

SC: After working with Robbie, and then seeing the movie, *The Last Waltz*, did you get a better idea of what made the band such a great act, or somehow give you some insight into Robbie as a musician?

GS: I wore the grooves off of their albums and remember playing "Up on Cripple Creek" endlessly. So, seeing the movie and being in the studio on the other side of the glass was a treat. By being the engineer and not the producer, and having most of those guys knowing I was also a musician, I was fortunate to hang out with them, and in some ways, was part of the brotherhood musicians have with each other.

SC: Was it like that working with Nicky Hopkins as well?

GS: I am telling you, the talented musicians were great because they all knew their role. It was a treat to work with them because they were so easy to work with. With some musicians without that level of talent, you'd be spending all day in the studio, thinking, "What am I doing here?" Then, when you finally get something, you were supposed to say, "Good job," when what you really wanted to say was, "Keep practicing."

Working with guys like Hopkins, Robertson, and Keltner was great because they knew their jobs, did it well, and did it quick. Even if we had to do overdubs or something, you didn't need to tell them where to come in—they knew already.

What I learned about running the machine was that you had a lot of power. You could adjust the headphone mix to get different things out of different artists. By turning up a musicians headphone mix, he would play quieter; while, if you turned it down, he would play louder. By adjusting the mix of the headphones, you could get different things out of the musician.

This came in handy because when Richard Perry said, "Get it louder," I could do it by simply lowering the headphone mix and adjusting in that fashion.

SC: So, sitting in the studio, listening to Nicky Hopkins' piano or Robertson's guitar, did you ever think, "Now I know what made 'She's A Rainbow' such a great song," or "Now I know why the guitar part on that song worked so well"?

GS: Oh yeah—all the time.

It also made me realize why I quit working as a musician. The cream always rises to the top because of their level of talent. I did a bunch of work with Lee Ritenour in the studio when he was young, and he's a huge jazz guy now. Back then, he was 16 and he would come in with this big grin, and we'd see this young kid just playing amazing guitar. I would think, "Holy shit, this is why I quit! How can someone that young be that good?"

I could practice my whole life and still not be as good as he was at 16. That was one of the great things about the job, though. Working with the world's most talented musicians was great because they could get it right with a minimum number of takes.

SC: Lets move on and talk about what it was like in the studio, and your involvement with recording two of the most iconic albums of all time: Fleetwood Mac's *Rumours* and Pink Floyd's *"The Wall"*. *Rumors* was recorded in 1976, right?

GS: That sounds right; I think it was in the summer. They had already recorded some things in Northern California and brought down the tapes for overdubs, sweetening, and whatnot. I worked very closely with Lindsey Buckingham, and he was really the driving force behind the album as far as mixing. He was almost maniacal about getting the best sounds he could for the album.

SC: By this time, *The Dark Side of the Moon* was a smash hit. As an engineer, was that the gold standard for recording and audio work?

GS: Completely—up until *The Wall* was released. The guy who engineered that was a genius [laughs]!

Yeah, *Dark Side* was a phenomenon and the album, in terms of sound and song quality, was something to shoot for. With *Rumours*, I not only remember working closely with Lindsey and his overseeing the details, but also the fact he married my secretary.

SC: He married your secretary?

GS: Yeah. While working, he would always joke with me, and say things like, "Sorry I took your secretary." It was like a running gag we would play with each other.

I remember one day—and this is something I think about from time to time—he mentioned that Christy McVie liked me, and Lindsey asked if I wanted to be set up with her. I am not sure why but I told him I had to go home and think about it. Not sure why I never pursued that. She was the nicest lady, though—not only her looks, but her personality as well...just a nice, nice lady.

I was in the middle of getting divorced at the time.

SC: You were still married to the girl you brought out from Kansas?

GS: Yeah. I think more of the reason I didn't pursue Christy [McVie] was my boss, Ed Cobb. When he gave me the job, he told me that I was in charge of all these bands, and all these groups, and that if I messed around, I was gone.

So, I came back and told Lindsey I couldn't do it. At the time, everyone in the band was banging everybody else, and it was a party-type atmosphere. As a matter of fact, when I first started working with Lindsey, he said, pointblank, "Everything you have ever heard about sex and drugs and Fleetwood Mac is true, and there is stuff you haven't even heard."

SC: Lindsey said that?

GS: Yeah, and the band wasn't hiding it or shy about it. It was wide open about what it was and at the time. I was kind of like, "Okay, cool," and still focused on trying to make the record.

I do remember joking with Lindsey one day, telling him, "I said no to Christie, but what about Stevie?" to which he just smiled and said, "Oh boy, oh boy...you will have to meet her." At that time, I hadn't met Stevie yet, because she hadn't come to the studio.

SC: Okay—I am glad you brought that up. One of the most widespread and widely known rumors in rock and roll is Stevie Nicks doing cocaine in her ass. When you look at some of the most mythic rock rumors, you have the Ozzy Osbourne bat-head thing, you've got all sorts of stuff about Rod Stewart, you have got the David Bowie/Mick Jagger rumor, and so on. In this case, you were an eyewitness to this specific event. What were the circumstances behind it?

GS: I actually didn't know the Stevie Nicks rumor was that well known, but I can tell you I was there. She would come into the studio and into the control room. She would be kind of weird and sit in the corner. She was actually kind of nasty to me. She was pretty, but she was also pretty difficult.

It had to have been maybe after a week, when I was working with Richard [Dashut] doing some mixing or whatever, and Lindsey came into the room and said to me, "You've got to deal with this."

I said, "I have to deal with what?"

Lindsey says, "You've got to get Stevie out of the bathroom. She is locked in the bathroom, and you have the key."

So, I get the key, and open the door...and this guy is doing coke up her ass. She has her dress up, bent over the sink, and he was blowing coke up her ass.

...And I had to be the one to say the party was over.

SC: What was their reaction?

GS: Believe it or not, they didn't really care that much. That rumor and that moment is 100% true. Once again, she and this guy didn't care that much. They simply came out of the bathroom and went back into the corner of the control room.

SC: That's amazing! The rumor itself was mysterious because of the fuzziness of the details. I heard everything from doing lines off her ass, to her taking coke in her ass, to guys sniffing coke out of her ass. This is fantastic, finally getting the truth behind the rumor.

GS: I asked Lindsey the next day, "Man, what was that all about?"

He told me that the membranes in her nose were so bad that it was the only way she could use coke. I just said, "Okay, I got it now." Of course, after working with Sly Stone, that seemed normal.

SC: At the time, you were still officially the studio manager, so you didn't actually receive a credit on *Rumours* for the work you did, correct?

GS: I haven't looked, to be honest. I thought I may have gotten a 2nd engineer credit, but the truth is that, in those days, I didn't really care. It was all in real time, and I didn't care if I got it or I didn't get it. I look back now because I was young and didn't realize the magnitude of the moment.

If it wasn't for Bill Schnee telling me to give my name to Richard Perry on *Goodnight, Vienna*, I probably would not have gotten my name on that. I remember going to Perry in the mastering lab to hand him my name to get the credit. Looking back, hell yeah I wished I had fought harder for a credit on *Rumours* and *The Wall*.

I know one thing: on *Rumours,* it was Richard Dashut who got the money.

SC: By working on *Rumours* and *Goodnight, Vienna,* did your own stock go up by being involved?

GS: Looking back, it absolutely did, though, at that time, I didn't realize it.

After *The Wall,* I realized how huge and how monumental it was. Why it took *The Wall* to help me realize that, and not *Rumours* or the work with Ringo and Carly, I am not sure.

SC: It sounds like, with *Rumours,* you and Lindsey were pretty close.

GS: Lindsey was great to work with. We worked together for close to a month and he was great. He and I really did the majority of the work on the album, and the fact was Richard [Dashut] was learning on the job. He [Richard] was open to learning, and he knew he didn't know, so I did a lot of the engineering work and probably should have been given an engineer's credit. I am not sure if he did any recording work after *Rumours,* but that's what happened on the *Rumours* album, specifically.

Once again, Lindsey ended up marrying my secretary.

SC: Are they still married?

GS: I don't know, but they were living off of 6th Street in LA at that time. He was a great guy, he was talented, he had a mission, and he was focused.

SC: Do you think he is underrated as a songwriter? If you had to give Lindsey a label, would it be guitarist or songwriter?

GS: I would say he was a great producer. He and I mixed that album. At that time, he was the man who put *Rumours* together, he made the decisions, and he made the call. He was very much to *Rumours* what Roger Waters was to *The Wall*. They were both the driving forces behind those albums, and without them, those albums would not exist.

SC: One last Fleetwood Mac question: based on the overwhelming popularity of *Rumours*, why was the follow up, *Tusk*, under-whelming? When you heard *Tusk*, what were your thoughts on it?

GS: They did some of the overdubs in the recording room, and while I did not work on that album, I heard from some of the people who had done some of the work on *Tusk*—so this is hearsay without question—but, in the recording circles, they said that Mick Fleetwood was more involved in *Tusk*, and Lindsey had not taken the extensive role that he took on *Rumours*.

Once again, this is second-hand because I did not work on the album, but after working with Lindsey and *Rumours*, and then listening to *Tusk*, it's obvious there were things on *Tusk* that Lindsey would never have done if he was overseeing the album in my opinion.

SC: So, you had a group of friends who were all engineers and whatnot who shared stories?

GS: Yeah, we would see each other around the city, BS over beers on what we were working on, and swap stories. No different, I guess, than a construction worker or some business guys do.

SC: Ken Caillait recently wrote a book about the *Rumours* album. After reading it, were your recollections similar to his?

GS: Yes and no. I thought from a technical perspective it was excellent and very accurate. Some of the other things in the book I disagreed with, or at least my memories of certain events contradicted some of his. I think it is like anything else, though, where people tend to remember things differently, and four different people will probably remember the same event in slightly different ways. Throw in the fact it was over 30 years ago, and there are bound to be some differences.

SC: Did you ever hear any stories about Phil Spector, John Lennon, and working on the *Rock and Roll* sessions?

GS: Once again, complete hearsay, but the word was that anything having to do with Phil Spector was always manic. I heard stories from other people about Phil, guns, and booze, so nothing surprises me. I never met him or worked with him, but you hear enough similar stories for a long enough time, coming from people you know and trust.

Word was he was just out right crazy. After seeing how Lennon was on the Ringo albums, and hearing what it was like to work with Spector, I could easily see how any work done between Lennon and Spector would have been a weird experience.

SC: Between *Rumours* and *The Wall*, were there any other notable projects you worked on?

GS: I do not remember any specific albums, but I worked on a lot of songs during that period. People would come in, just to do a couple of songs or maybe a specific song. We did a lot of work with Richard Perry Productions, and we did some songs for Alice Cooper and his guitarist, Dick Wagner.

I remember working with Alice, and I had this image of him as this crazy devil-guy or something, because that was his stage persona.

Then, he finally comes in, I get to meet him, and he is this Republican guy with bourbon or something. He was very together, very professional, and all business.

It was a total surprise for me—I was expecting something totally crazy.

When we worked with his guitarist, Dick Wagner, I was working on the recording of his album. One night, we were working late. I was working the board, and there was this folded up paper by one of the controls. I was into the project, and didn't know what it was, so I just swatted it off the board, and the whole place went quiet.

It turns out that was their coke that I had just dumped on the floor.

I didn't even know! I was just doing my job and working the controls. So, we have this black console that is covered with white powder, and Dick Wagner comes over with a rolled-up bill, and they start snorting the cocaine that was showered across the board. I was no angel, but when I was in the room, I kept it all business. The industry is littered with guys who were drunk or drugged-up, and screwed up a session who never got to work in the business again.

SC: Because you never took drugs or drank while working in the studio, how exactly did the effects of drugs and alcohol effect performers and musicians?

GS: I can remember one band that came in to record. They took a break, and they had this grocery bag filled with coke and they would put their whole heads in and snort away. Their faces were all white and covered with coke, but after that, they couldn't record anything and were useless. Guys who were doing coke could never perform, and you could rarely get anything out of them. I don't remember their name, but, once again, more often than not, the guys drinking or getting high in the studio rarely could perform...with Jim Keltner being the one big exception.

SC: Lets talk about *The Wall*. How did you get the job, and what were your thoughts when you first heard you were going to be working with Pink Floyd?

GS: Here's a back story.

I was working with AVI and running the place. We were one of the innovators of disco, and I was working from 7 p.m. to 7 a.m., all night long, making dance records. We were the first to invent the long, giant singles, and the reason we invented them was because The Mastering Lab, which was located behind Producers Workshop, helped us figure out how to do it.

That came about because we were doing a lot of work with a band called San Tropez and some other different disco acts. They were giving us feedback that they wanted more highs, they wanted more bottom-end, more bass or more drums, and the records were selling big time.

I think we were one of the first—if not the first—to create drum loops.

I would make my own drum loops by recording a drum track on a quarter inch two-track recorder of about four bars, splice it together to make a loop, and then used a weight on the tape hanging off the side, hit play, and record a drum track that just kept going over and over again.

I would then record this onto a 24-track machine in stereo for however long the song was supposed to be. We didn't have drum machines back then. So, I talked to Doug Sax, owner of The Mastering Lab, and he said the sound was all based on the size of the groove speed and some other things, and mentioned how putting a single onto a 12-inch would give better sound quality.

We did it, and the clubs went nuts.

Pink Floyd was using both studios at the time, and that's when I met Bob Ezrin. Once again, I was running the studio by day, and recording these disco songs at night, so it was a busy time.

I knew Bob because he would call me and let me know what he needed when he was working in the studio, and he would typically work both rooms.

SC: So, you knew Bob from his previous work, and knew a bit about him and his style?

GS: Oh yeah. He called me up in late July of 1978 and told me some of the story.

Floyd had already been working on the album for almost a year, but a large portion of the album was redone in August through September of '78. Before then, during the day, I was dealing with Bob Ezrin, making sure he got what he needed, while still recording disco at night. Bob Ezrin knew I was the go-to guy.

Come to think of it, Pink Floyd was in the studio a month or so earlier, so I saw them here and there in the studio. I remember I wasn't getting a lot of sleep at that time. This one night, I managed to get to bed—and I was sleeping *well*—and the phone rings.

It wasn't uncommon to get a late night call for something studio-related—like if something broke, or someone had a question about the control board—but this call was Bob Ezrin. I remember the call to this day:

He said, "Hi, this is Bob."

"Hi Bob; what's up?"

"Do you get paid by the hour, or monthly, or what?"

"I get paid by the month," I said.

"Roger [Waters] wants to talk to you tomorrow. I think he wants to interview you, and if you get it, I'll pay you by the hour. He wants to meet at 10 a.m."

So, I go into the studio at 10 a.m., and I see James Guthrie there in the mix room. He was the one who mixed the whole album. There was this engineer from Canada named Brian Richardson, and he was the guy I was going to replace. I later find out that Brian and Roger got into a big fight, and Roger said he couldn't work with him anymore.

So, I walk into the studio, and Roger says, "How ya doing, mate?" and we shake hands and whatever. Roger says, "I've got a question for you: if I wanted to invert the bass and make it sound like drums, what would you say to me?"

I said, "If you've got the time and money, let's do it."

Roger simply said, "You're hired."

He didn't want to hear no, and that was it. Bob [Ezrin] later told me that Brian would always say "you can't do this" or "you can't do that," so hearing me say, "I could do anything with time and money," was the perfect answer for Roger to hear at that time. He wanted a guy who would just say, "Let's do it." You would have some engineers or board guys who were more into electronics or techies, who were aware of the limitations, whereas I was a guy who did anything necessary and whatever it took to get the sound I wanted.

So, I met with Bob, and he had set up a trailer outside of the studio he was using as his offices. He said, "Here is the deal: we are starting today, and the schedule is 20 hours on, four hours off. We need to get this album done. We are re-cutting almost the entire record, and we have to get it to Columbia by September 1st."

That was in May of 1977, which basically meant we had four months to re-cut and retool the entire album. Bob got me $50 bucks an hour, though, so working 20 hours a day was great money.

SC: That's still great money by today's standards.

GS: It was the most money I had ever made in my life.

SC: So, you are making great money, and working with Pink Floyd at the height of their fame. That had to be your finest hour.

GS: Well, as always, I was there for the moment. Looking back, I wasn't nearly as excited as I probably should have been. Basically, Bob said, "You are with Roger Waters—do whatever he wants you to do."

Guthrie was living in the mixing room, and I basically sat next to Roger and helped him do whatever he wanted to get done. So, Roger would say, "I want to record this whole track, I want to re-record this bass, I want this track with more pop," and so forth. Then, towards the end, we spent major time recording all of the sound effects.

This was long before CDs of MP3s full of sound effects came around. If you wanted to record a sound effect, you had to go out and get it. The baby crying, the phone, the plane…we recorded all of that stuff. One of the most memorable things was doing the solo on "Another Brick in the Wall (pt 2)".

SC: Classic song and a huge hit. I remember it well when I was in the 7th and 8th grade. It was only later, when I was 15 or 16, when I heard the entire album and realized the brilliance.

GS: That was one of the few times I wasn't working with Roger, but working with David [Gilmour], and it took about five days. David had every guitar and amp you could think of in the studio. Any combination you wanted was available. Thousands and thousands of dollars worth of equipment: Marshall, Vox, Fender…you name, it he had it.

We were working with a 16-track and 24-track we had synced together. Gilmour basically used 12-tracks on the 16-track recorder to play whatever he felt like playing for the solo. He was using the 16-track recorder, which meant he recorded about 12 different solos. The next day, he came back, reviewed each and every take, and he would say, "I want that lick," or, "I like that part," and for each part that he liked, we would bounce it to an open track.

So, we had this one track, with nothing but the parts he liked, and he wanted to use those parts as a guide track. Once he got the solo worked out with the parts he liked, we wiped all of the other tracks, and he would take a Les Paul through a Marshall using all treble, or a Strat through a Vox using all bass, and all these different combinations playing the same solo using the same guide track. Then, we would just listen to the different combos, and blend all of the tracks together, which gave the amazing sound you hear on that solo.

Later, guys would come in and ask to get the sound David Gilmour had on that song, and I would laugh out loud and tell them, "You don't have the money to get that sound." It was funny, and it was true. That was the power of that unique sound we were able to capture for that solo. I think—from start to finish—we worked on that solo for four or five days.

SC: Many people consider *The Wall* to be the last true incarnation of Pink Floyd, as Rick Wright was fired after the album's completion, and he didn't really contribute too much. Did you get a sense of the turmoil or disharmony between the band, or get a sense of the inner strife between any of them?

GS: Truth be told, I didn't, and that was mainly because, when I worked on *The Wall*, it was just Roger and I, or David and I. The only time I was in the studio with all of them was at the completion of the record, and we were listening to the final product.

SC: So, Waters, Gilmour, Rick Wright, Nick Mason are all in the studio listening to the final version of *The Wall* with Bob Ezrin?

GS: That's right. There were some other guys there—James Guthrie I think was in there as well.

There was beer, and it was a really loose atmosphere, actually. To me, it looked like they were all getting along, but, once again, it was like a party-type vibe with beer and pot. It was the only time I saw any of those guys drinking or smoking and relaxing. I knew Bob Ezrin was doing a lot of coke. He offered it to me on occasion, but I never took any.

SC: So, in the studio, they were pros?

GS: Oh yeah. Like I said, I never saw them doing anything until the final listening of the master tape.

I remember, as we were listening to the last couple of songs on Side 4, they were all pretty loaded by that time. Bob Ezrin looks at me and says, "I'm going to bust your ass. We are going to take 15-20 seconds out of the end of the album where the wall is falling down, I am going to give you the edit points, and we're going to do it right now."

The band was all laughing, thinking I was going to blow it and not be able to get his edit points he wanted, and I was a bit nervous, because that was a lot of pressure. Fortunately, I had an old stopwatch that I kept with me, so I put it on my side and below where the rest of the people in the studio couldn't see it. Using the stopwatch, I hit the mark perfectly.

Bob and the band couldn't believe I was able to hit the mark. Bob and Roger were asking, "How the hell did you do that?" I just smiled and laughed. I never told them how I was able to hit the mark. I think that sold them on my abilities [laughs]. It also reinforced why smoking and drinking in the studio for engineers was a risky proposition, though.

SC: At what point where you were listening to *The Wall* did you realize this album was going to be an incredible hit and a revolutionary piece of music? What was the first song you heard?

GS: When I heard the chorus to "Another Brick in the Wall (Pt 2)" with the "We don't need no education" part, I knew that it was going to be a smash, because that hook just stayed with you and resonated. It had the magic. Want another story that may dispel a rumor about that song?

SC: Sure! We've dispelled a few already, so let's add another to our list.

GS: Well, if you look it up, the story goes that the kids on that song were from England, and they claimed they were owed royalties and there was some big controversy.

That's wrong, because I was there when they recorded it.

They brought in the Hollywood Children's Choir—a children's church choir. Bob Ezrin brought them in. This is how good of a producer Bob was: he brought them in, taught them the part, and then got them to sing with an English accent. He got them to do that and was able to get that out of them. We recorded that there in Hollywood. Now, the English version of that part was there on the demo, but we re-recorded it in Hollywood.

SC: Another myth exposed!

GS: Yeah, he didn't pay them anything. Bob was great like that. For one song, I remember he brought in bagpipes and started calling everybody "Sandy" while talking in a Scottish accent for some strange reason. But that is the brilliance of Bob: he was great at getting everyone in the right frame of mind and set the right type of mood.

There was another time when were working, though, when Nick Mason came in, and I didn't see him much, but he apparently said something that Bob didn't like, and Bob slammed him against the studio wall and told him he would never work again—or let him in the studio again or something like that.

Bob wasn't afraid to take control when he had to. When you are dealing with huge bands like that, you had to take control. We used to play little games in the studio as well. Bud Wyatt was gone by then, so they hired some guy from San Francisco who thought he knew everything.

We were working one day, and Bob started hearing a rattle coming from one of the Altec speakers. He shut down the session and told everyone to go to lunch while the new guy was going to fix the speaker. We get back from lunch and start listening to the tape again, when Bob says, "Stop."

Bob goes over to the speaker, puts his fist through it, and tells this guy, "I told you to fix it—not to move it," because this guy thought Bob wouldn't hear the rattle again if he just moved the speaker from the right side to the left. Bob had amazing ears.

SC: Would you say Bob was the George Martin of the time?

GS: He probably was the closest thing to George Martin that I ever worked with. From all of the people I worked with in the studio, he was the best.

SC: Apart from "Another Brick in the Wall (Pt2)", were you aware of the many other iconic songs on *The Wall*, and did you get a sense of how powerful they were? What were you thinking when you heard "Comfortably Numb" for the first time?

GS: Funny you should mention that.

We finally got down to the mixing of the record—and I didn't mix it, because I was still working side-by-side with Roger. Finally, after four months of 20 on and four off, there were nights where we did nothing but listen to the album. On the side that "Comfortably Numb" is on, the sequence on the record is different than it is listed on the record jacket. I was listening to it at 3- or 4 a.m., and Roger asked me what I thought.

I told him I thought "Comfortably Numb" was in the wrong place on the album. I told him I thought it was such a great song, that it was out of place on that side of the album and it should be moved. He gave me kind of a nasty look, and we didn't talk too much about it. The next day, we get into the studio and he came up to me first thing and said, "Fucking mate! Guess what! You are right—we're moving it."

SC: So, on original pressings of *The Wall*, the track listing was as it was originally supposed to be, but after your two cents, you got Roger Waters to move "Comfortably Numb"?

GS: Yeah. If you count them out and look at the songs, then look at the track listing on the cover, they are different. The reason was that because they had to have the album done by September 1st, they had all of the covers and sleeves already printed—which is another reason why some copies of *The Wall* still list Brian Richardson as the engineer. No one got around to giving them my name for that credit.

So, we got to the end, and Bob came up to me and apologized for not having my name on the album. He promised that they would get it corrected on future versions, but it never happened. That was the business, though, so it wasn't surprising. The record companies are paying for sleeves and redesigns and they weren't going to pay a cent more to make a change to the sleeve to reward some engineer.

Later, I went to the release party at Columbia Records with Roger Waters, and we are there with all of the label's muckity-mucks and all that. Roger tells the guy personally that I should have my name on the jacket and the guy just nods and says, "yeah, yeah, yeah," but it never happened.

SC: So, if you saw Roger today, and asked him about not getting your name on the album, would he know what you were talking about?

GS: Of course he would! We spent a lot of time together on that album, so absolutely. At the end, Bob told me he would write a letter on my behalf, but I was just kind of, "Meh, don't bother."

I do want to say that half of those effects on the album came by accident, and that's what I remember about working with Roger. We would use an acoustic and a guide vocal to lay down a basic work track, so if he liked the guitar, he would ask me to boost and add effects, and we would sit, track-by-track, and take what we had existing and tweak it, and add this and that to get these amazing sounds.

From that angle, a lot of *The Wall* started really organic in nature. The segue-ways between the songs on the album are what really made it, though, and that was the genius of Roger. We also used the adage, "When in doubt, leave it out," which meant there were probably some pretty cool things we did that wound up on the floor of the editing room.

SC: Imagine what you could do with the master tapes as some type of re-release.

GS: Oh yeah, we had hours and hours of stuff on the tapes. They could probably release it as a lost mix, or director's cut, or something like that, and make millions.

Another story; half way through the sessions, I was sitting with Bob in his trailer, and he was asking how I was doing, and telling me

Roger was happy with my work and all that. He then asks how I am holding up with the 20-hour days, and I tell him I am doing fine.

He then opens up and tells me the reason for the September push was that if the album was completed by September, he was to be given a $2 million dollar cash bonus.

I mean, it was 1978 and he was getting $2 million in cash. So, then, as we are wrapping up the project, Bob says, "I've got one more assignment for you. Tomorrow, I am going to have a guard install a red phone on a table in front of the vault, where we kept all of the masters."

Back then, you'd have 40 takes, and Roger would always be trying different mixes, so the studios had a librarian who handled all of the master tapes. So, he had me sitting all day in front of the vault with this red phone.

Finally, the phone rings, and it's Bob, who says, "I've got $2 million dollars, a .357 in my briefcase, and I am on a plane to London. See you in a year." Next thing I know, the guys from Columbia come and pick up the masters.

SC: Amazing what a different time it was when it came to air travel.

GS: It was a different era, for sure. There's one last thing I remember about *The Wall* that a lot of Floyd people are interested in.

I mentioned Roger doing the segue-ways. We listened to the whole record with the EQs and the levels and all of that. We get to Side 4, I think we are done, and Roger says, "I've got an idea."

All I could think was, "Oh no!" because I thought we were done and we were listening to the final masters. He said, "Hook me a line to the studio and run me a line back. We are going to record one last thing that you are going to edit and add to the record."

So, we are listening to the final notes of the little music part on Side 4, and Roger said into the mic, "Isn't this where we came in?"

He had me cut it right between "isn't this where" and "we came in" and had me edit the "isn't this where" to the end of the Side 4, and the "we came in" to beginning of Side 1. He did it just because he knew that someday, someone would splice it. Of course, now they do all that stuff digitally, but it was just another one of the things that made Roger "Roger." That was the last thing we did on the record.

SC: So, that whole bit from the end of Side 4 connecting to the start of Side 1 was just you and Roger Waters?

GS: Yeah. We were mastering and making the acetates, and that was when he got the idea. If someone was to pull up the original mix, that snippet is not on there because we added that on the fly. Later, I got a digital copy of *The Wall* that made me sick. Whoever mixed the digital copy just did an outright horrible job. I literally threw my headphones down. I am sure Roger was pissed.

SC: So, that was it with working with Roger?

GS: No, he came back to me and said he was planning on doing a live show. He asked some of the other engineers and I to help him run the effects for the concert. They were one of the first to run tape effects and stuff. It was at the Sports Center, and at one show, the fireworks started a fire.

I met Mick Jagger there as well. It was something.

SC: Were you working the soundboard for the original Los Angeles *Wall* concerts?

GS: Yeah. We had all of the effects set up, and the job was to push the tape button at the right time to coordinate the sound with the effect. I went to Roger's last concert, and he still does the same thing.

SC: Did he give you tickets?

GS: No, I had to go get the tickets myself. It's hard to get past management, and it was so long ago and all that stuff.

SC: It sounds like he liked your work—did you ever work with him again on "The Final Cut" or some of his early solo work?

GS: No, I never worked with him again after that. I think he recorded some of those other projects over in England or something. The thing is, if I ever got a chance to meet him and joked about the missing credit on *The Wall*, he would know exactly who I was. When you spend four months and 20 hours a day with a guy....

SC: We should call in next time he is on *Rockline* or something like that.

GS: Yeah, we should. That would be pretty funny, actually.

SC: Were there any other projects from the 70s?

GS: After that, a lot of my work was dance and disco and all of that stuff. It was a transitional period after that, and though it paid well, it wasn't the same. The 70s were the peak for recording when you look at the quality of the songs and the albums. Then, we transitioned into the 80s, and it got worse.

SC: Were you even a Pink Floyd fan before working with them?

GS: Actually, I wasn't. I was familiar with them, but it wasn't like it was with The Beatles and whatnot.

SC: When you heard the first notes on the solo, did you at least get a chill?

GS: There were a lot of moments on *The Wall* that were amazing, but there were so many great songs and moments that you did not have time to digest some of them.

Remember, with $2 million on the line, you didn't really have time to bask in the moment. It was finish one thing, and move on to the next.

I talked with Bob a year later, and we hung out, but I didn't pressure him about the credit or anything...once again, I was in the moment.

SC: You are like the Forest Gump of engineering.

GS: In a way, I guess I was. It goes back to the point, though, where it was a job I was getting paid for, and it literally was just going to work, like a plumber or something. I still remember, "If you can't eat your meat, you can't finish your pudding."

SC: How did that line come about?

GS: They were always joking around and saying things in the studio.

SC: So, that was just something goofy they would say in the studio?

GS: Oh yeah. Some of them were just random stuff, and that was one that just kind of stuck. Everyone kept repeating that line in particular, so we went with it. A lot of the stuff on *The Wall* was interesting. Getting the clips of the phone call, the helicopter, and all of that stuff...

SC: All of those sounds were recorded specifically for *The Wall?*

GS: Yeah. The helicopter sound, the plane, and all of that we got from the airports. We would get the tape, and then get back to the studio to work the fade-ins and fade-outs.

SC: Looking back now, out of all the musicians you worked with, where do Waters and Gilmour rank?

GS: I thought Waters was a genius. He worked it out as he went, but he knew what he wanted, and it was just a matter of how he was going to get there. He was a lot like Lindsey Buckingham on *Rumours*, where each had a vision and an idea of what they wanted, and they were going to get it no matter what it took.

With Gilmour, it was all about his guitar playing. He could get more out of one note than any other player I have ever seen. The tone, the feel, and the nuances of his playing...it was powerful.

SC: It's amazing how, on these later albums, even though they were credited as a group, it was always one guy with an amazing vision.

GS: Agreed. I could also see how, with a talented individual working within a context of a band, that friction gets created.

In The Beatles, for instance, you had two guys with that vision, which I could see created problems. John Lennon would bitch about Paul McCartney non-stop. At that point in time, you could really tell that he hated McCartney, and he made it clear. Lennon was not happy.

SC: Are you disappointed you never got a chance to work with Paul McCartney?

GS: Sure. Like John Lennon, he was one my idols. And though he contributed to Ringo's albums, I never saw him in the studio. I liked a lot of McCartney's solo albums. I thought *Band on the Run* was excellent for the production, but, then again, the solo album he did with just him on a four-track recorder I liked as well.

SC: So you could probably almost hear in McCartney's solo albums—with him being a perfectionist—it would have really rubbed Lennon the wrong way. After working with John, did the whole Lennon/McCartney feud kind of make sense?

GS: When he [Lennon] went off on me about *Yellow Submarine*, these guys were on a pedestal. When he told me about hating the film and the budget troubles he had with the movie, it was an eye-opener for me that someone told John Lennon, "No". I thought Lennon could snap his finger and do whatever, so that, as far as realizing about the industry and stuff like that, it was a true insight into the world of stardom.

SC: After that, you figure if someone can tell John Lennon "No," when somebody says "No" to you, its not that bad—simply part of the industry.

GS: Oh yeah. By that same token, after working with Lennon, it also gave me a "you can do this" type moment, where I gained a lot of confidence in my ability.

SC: When you look back at your discussion with John about *Yellow Submarine*, do you ever wish you would have said something like, "I had a delicious grilled cheese sandwich for dinner last night?"

GS: I have a feeling no matter what I said, he would have exploded, and I kind of felt like it was a setup, with no response being the right one. Then again, I was happy and on cloud nine just to have him acknowledge me.

SC: Years later, when you read more about Lennon, and you realized he had an acerbic wit and style, and that things like that were common, did it make you feel better?

GS: Yeah. It made me feel better knowing it was just Lennon being Lennon. I could see how, with someone who was emotional or something like that, he could be a nightmare. At the end of the day, though, it was an honor to work with him, and all of the great musicians and people I worked with in the 70s.

SC: At that time, John Lennon and Ringo were hanging out with Harry Nilson producing some of his albums. Did you ever work with him?

GS: I did one record with Harry. Actually, "we attempted to do a record with Harry" would be a better description.

I can't even remember what the title was, but I got hired to help record it. They had rented out a huge studio in Burbank, and their plan was to record live in the studio with Harry, a 52-piece orchestra, and this big production.

Nilson was a big name, and having to organize and set up recording for that many people was a challenge under any circumstance. With Harry's reputation, we kind of had an idea there may be some unforeseen circumstances.

The room was huge, so it was the biggest production I had ever done. I set up the percussion, the wind instruments and all that stuff was ready to go.

Seven o'clock comes around—there is no Harry. Fifteen minutes go by, and still no Harry.

The producer—I can't remember his name—calls a break, and one of the funny things about working with orchestras was that during breaks, the string players would always play cards, while all of the horn players would go out and smoke pot.

Anyhow, finally, word rolls around that Harry is in the studio, so all the musicians go back to their seats and get ready to roll, but after a few more minutes, he still isn't in the studio. I go to find him, and as I turn the corner, I see Harry walking up the hall, pushing a dolly with all of these cases of sake. He then sees me, and he is obviously drunk, because he is talking very slowly and slurring, and says, "Sake for everybody."

He then wheels the dolly into the room, and everybody starts drinking sake and getting completely ripped, and nothing at all gets recorded from the sessions. I later heard that it cost RCA, who was paying for it all, $30,000 trying to get that session done. That was the last time I ever worked with Harry...or *almost* worked with Harry.

SC: Recording live is probably tough with just four or five guys, so with the full orchestra, it was probably an enormous undertaking, right?

GS: The more you have to record, the more challenging it is.

I later worked with The Crusaders on a tour of Europe and Asia, and got to record them with BB King for an album called *The Royal Jam*, and I have a lot of great stories from that album and that tour as well. They were big in jazz, and had a female singer named Randy Crawford. The Asia and European tour alone could probably fill a book, and I will get into details of that whole episode later.

SC: In the book, Making *Rumours*, Ken Caillat talks extensively about the recording process for the *Rumours* album. Having read the book, what were your thoughts on it, and do you agree or disagree with some of Caillat's observations?

GS: I liked the book and it was an interesting read. As for as being able to confirm or deny, I can only say I was involved in the mixing process, so I can't speak about some of the other stuff in the book. I can say that Caillat was known as a good engineer, and he did describe the process of mixing well.

To set the record completely straight, he talks about David Lebarre, but I knew him then as David Barre. At that time, in the studio, you always had a maintenance engineer, which was a very important position. However, David Lebarre did not build the room at Producers Workshop as described in the book. The person that built the room was Bud Wyatt. I would not be surprised if Lebarre told people he built the room, but I can tell you—without question—that Bud Wyatt built specific room.

I don't want to rag on Lebarre, but the fact was that he was not well-liked. He came from San Francisco and had an attitude. I know firsthand, because I was the studio manager, and the Carol Harris he talked about in the book was my secretary and the person I hired to help me with the day-to-day functions of the studio.

At that time, I was running the studio, doing engineer work; and at nights, I was working with AVI, making disco records. Truth be told, I did not see Caillat or [*Rumours* co-producer] Richard Dashett that often, as they were doing their work on a different schedule than I was. The moment in time at which I became involved with the project was during one night, when I got a call from Ed Cobb from AVI, who said Lindsey [Buckingham] wanted to remix the album.

That happened all of the time—an artist wanted to do some remixing—so it wasn't uncommon. It was not a big deal at all—certainly not a slam on Caillat or his ability as an engineer. When I met Lindsey, he was explicit when he said that myself, Lindsey, and Richard Dashett were going to remix the album, but Richard was learning on the job, and needed some help, but was going to get full royalties and credit for the job as payback for his support: letting the band live at his house over the last year.

Lindsey asked if I was okay with that—which I was—because I was on full salary, and whatever they wanted to do, I would do. At this time, I wasn't even really familiar with the group. They were not superstars yet—they were basically a new group to me.

Lindsey was cool and great to work with, though, and we ended up remixing the whole album. When you are an engineer, you are not allowed to make production decisions unless given permission to make those decisions.

So, Lindsey, Richard, and myself sat down, and part of that job was to make the production decisions to remove tracks and overdubs from the mix, as Lindsey thought there were too many on it. I can't swear to it that additional mixing decisions were made after we did our mix of the album, but I *can* tell you that, when I hear the album, I can hear what we did. We spent more than half of our time or more taking things out, and Lindsey admitted that he was the biggest culprit, and that the mix sounded way too busy with too many guitar parts.

That is why the final mix sounds so good: you've got your bass, your guitar, your drums, your keyboards, and the vocals. Lindsey analyzed a lot of it and moved certain licks to the turnarounds and little things like that during the re-mixing process, because he wanted to—in his own words—"get to the heart of the song."

Once again, the final mix that Caillat worked on was very different than the finished product. Let me be clear: I am not slamming him, because he was an excellent engineer and producer, and last-minute mixing changes happened all the time. My work with Roger Waters on *The Wall* is a testament to that. If Lindsey wanted to make changes and production decisions, he was going to have the final word, and that's exactly what happened.

The end result was really good, and it was an amazing album.

SC: Caillat also wrote in his book that Lindsey could be erratic and prone to mood swings. Did you ever see that? At points in the book, it almost makes Lindsey look like a monster at times.

GS: Lindsey was a great guy to me. I never witnessed him get violent, mean, or angry at all. I know there were some things in the book about Lindsey abusing Carol on their way towards divorce, as well.

While that is certainly possible, during my time working with Lindsey, he was great to work alongside and he was a total pro. Out of that whole experience, Stevie Nicks with the bathroom incident was really the one that stood out as having some issues.

I still can't believe I missed my chance to date Christie McVie. She was a really sweet lady. At the end of the day, I can say he [Caillat] mastered the record, but you know your mixes, because you would know when tracks are missing. Now, as producer, he may have had permission to make those changes.

SC: So, it is possible that Caillat and Lindsey both made the decision to strip down the mix, and Caillat for whatever reason, took a step back and let Lindsey, Richard, and yourself handle that process?

GS: That is a possibility. If I had to make a guess, and knowing what happens in the studio between artists and producers, I would think it likely that Lindsey asked Caillat not to show up, and Lindsey would take it on himself, because there was probably some conflict as to who was running the show.

I say this because, when you read that chapter in the book about the original mix, he talks about how Lindsey and Mick Fleetwood would continually say how good the original mix sounded and whatnot. If they heard it and thought it sounded good, it's a bit of a conflicting story, knowing that I worked shoulder-to-shoulder with Lindsey remixing it again.

Hopefully, in the history of that album, this will help set the record straight or at least add some information that can be used for historical context. Looking back, I should have fought much harder to have my name put on all of these projects, but I was still making good money, and in the moment, when you are making good money, you are more content, and not thinking about future royalties, credits, and whatnot.

SC: I asked you this about your work on *The Wall*, but when you were mixing *Rumours*, did you immediately know it was going to be a great album? Or, were there songs you heard that you knew were going to be an immediate hit? What were you thinking in the studio?

GS: Truth be told, I was so focused on doing my job. I didn't really have the luxury to think about the songs or judge their quality.

When you are in the studio, it is some demanding work. I saw a list of stressful jobs once, and studio engineer was second only behind air traffic controller, and I believe it! It is non-stop "raise this, lower that, remove this, bounce that, go back," and more.

Like I said, apart from Bob Ezrin's trailer, I rarely saw drugs or alcohol being abused in the studio. That said, knowing the stresses of the job, and the money involved, it was easy to see how that lifestyle could lead to abuse.

For *Rumours*, it was only Stevie Nicks doing drugs. Lindsey was always in control, and I realized that, as we were making our changes, the mixes kept getting better and better. For the song "Dreams" specifically, it was a far better song when Lindsey and I were done with the mixing—or re-mixing would be a better word.

This happened a lot on *The Wall* as well. We all worked with the adage of, "When in doubt, leave it out," which was ironic, given all of the production that went on for that record. Same with Steely Dan and *Aja*—Donald Fagan was very good about selecting and removing some of the tracks that were overkill.

Back to your original question, the one time I remember in the studio, in which everyone knew something special was happening, was Carly Simon's *Mockingbird*. Everyone in that studio—from the producers, the engineers, the musicians and anyone who was there—felt that it was something special, and knew, without a doubt, it was good stuff, and going to be a hit.

SC: So, it is the late 70's or early 80's, you finish *The Wall*—what happens next in your career?

GS: In '79, I was doing really well for myself as an engineer by day and producer of disco records at night, so I was considering going independent and doing all of my own stuff. I wanted to move away from having to do what they told me to do, and take more control of the process.

SC: Now, were you building a reputation, and were your services becoming more in demand? Was the phone ringing off the hook?

GS: I was getting a lot of calls to my home office, but because I was under contract with Liberace and AVI, I couldn't just jump ship. The management at AVI and Ed Cobb were cool, they were good, and they knew what was going on.

The word was out on the streets that I was a good engineer, so the phone was ringing. One day, I got a call from Ed, who said he was a friend of the manager of a band called The Jazz Crusaders. They had just done a record for MCA records called *Street Life*. He confided in me that the sax player, Wilton Felder, was the guy who usually mixed and produced their albums.

Felder was the really straight, Jehova's Witness, no-nonsense guy. Felder had submitted six different mixes of the *Street Life* album to MCA, and every one of them got rejected. So, Ed told me that I earned the shot to produce and mix the *Street Life* album without any oversight, and that I had total control to do whatever I wanted with the mix.

SC: So, you had never met anyone in The Crusaders at all, but were given the tapes and told to go ahead and do whatever needs to be done to get the album to be released?

GS: That is exactly what happened. I had made enough of a name in the industry, and that was the first real break I had to do producing. It was like an audition, in some regards, but I just looked at it like any other job and went to work. MCA loved it, and it felt good knowing my work was accepted.

Once again, I was making all of these disco records at that time, and I had done so much work cutting songs onto 12-inch disks that MCA asked me to make an extended 12-inch mix of *Street Life*.

That was a challenge, because, doing dance records, you then had to cut a loop to keep the rhythm and beat consistent. Now, doing all of that stuff is easy because it is digital, but back then, it was work. If you wanted to add a little guitar part to the end of the song, it was far harder. Another problem was that their tempo changed throughout the same song—not enough to hear if you were listening from start to finish—but it was clearly audible when cutting the extended mixes.

SC: So, with a longer song, the slight changes in tempo were small and unnoticeable, but, when editing and looping, they became far more apparent?

GS: That's right. The longer the song was, the more changes that happened. They are slight, but you could hear those changes when editing, and *Street Life*—at eight minutes long—was a challenge.

So, what I did was use the variable speed oscillator, or VSO, that controlled the motor. Now, in ProTools, it is easy; but back then, the only way to match those changes was by using the VSO to manually control the motor of the tape console. We made the extended mix, and it was huge.

A lot of those mixes were huge in Europe, but, at that time, there was a change in the industry, as the studios were shying away from big-budget productions, cutting budgets, and really pairing down the record productions.

The Wall may have marked the last album with that type of artistic control and huge budgets, and that was another reason I wanted to go out on my own. It was a time where they stopped caring about the sound and all of the things we worked hard to get sound-wise; the studios simply stopped being concerned with it.

Anyhow, Ed called and said The Crusaders loved my work on the album, and wanted to meet me and talk with me about it. So I go and meet Wilton, Joe, and Sticks.

SC: What was their reaction to meeting you?

GS: Wilton was cold—that was just the way he was. He was always stiff and straight. I'm not sure if it was because he was a Jehovah's Witness or what, but he was always tense and could never relax. Joe Sample was great, though. He is a superstar in the jazz world now, but he was really cool.

Anyhow, they said they liked my work with *Street Life* and wanted me to go on tour with them, handling the sound on their live East Coast tour they were going on. So, I gave my notice at the studio, and began transitioning into more live and production work with The Crusaders.

So, we rehearse and go on tour, and are a bit into it and things are going well, when we get a message that a meeting was called. We go to the meeting, and learn that The Crusaders were booked to do a European tour and scheduled to start in London.

I had never been to Europe, and the whole production was all first-class. I remember we were on a big 747 with the second floor and all of that, and we were drinking and smoking pot. On one of those flights, I remember drinking with the stewardess and the pilot. It was a different time, for sure.

SC: So your first gig is in London—what was the story?

GS: They were going to do two records: one in London, at the Royal Festival Hall with the Royal Philharmonic Orchestra; and one with BB King, called *The Royal Jam*. We were syncing together two 24-track machines, and we were picking the best tracks. I was really in my element.

On the first day, we were setting up the stage. It was tough with the full band, an orchestra, BB King, and BB's band. For a recording engineer, it was a real challenge. BB's band walks out, and says they don't want to be on that side of the stage, and that they would rather play on the other side and ask to move their stuff over. The stage guy comes out, and it starts getting heated, with him arguing with BB's band, and finally, they ask me to settle it. So, I figured this is BB's call, as he is the headliner, and we bring him out, as both sides are arguing their cases.

BB was so cool. He was standing there with his arms crossed, listening to both sides, and finally, he says to his band, "When the boss says 'do it', we do it—and he's the boss."

He pointed to me and walked off the stage without saying anything else. It was a relief, because moving his band would have been a nightmare. BB was great like that—easiest guy in the world to work with.

So, after London, we went to Paris, through Copenhagen, and then took trains all over Europe and even through Check Point Charlie in East Berlin.

SC: How did the recording in London come off?

GS: Two 24-track recorders, with full orchestration, with two bands, having to mic it all up, and balance all of the levels was tough. It was overwhelming, and the console took so much room…then, making matters worse, working with the British was challenging.

They are all gone when you want them—you would turn around to ask someone to do something and they would be gone. Then, they would show up an hour later, and say they went out for half pint of Bitter. They were nice guys, but you could just never count on them when you needed them to do the work, so basically, you were doing it all by yourself. We managed to get it done, but working with the Brits was challenging, to say the least.

SC: You managed to get it recorded, though?

GS: The shows came off great, and the machines worked well. We were using the industry-standard two-inch tape, and the syncing of the machines worked better than I thought it would.

Keep in mind; this was 1979 or 1980, so that was cutting-edge for the time. We were there for a week, and while I was there, the manager of Level 42, who was a newer group at the time, contacted me. They had heard of me and they wanted to meet, so that was cool.

I ended up meeting the manager and the two brothers. They liked my work on *Street Life*, and they asked if I would mix one of their records. So, when I wasn't prepping for the live shows with BB King and The Crusaders, I was doing work with Level 42.

We hit it off, and they invited me to a show they were playing in Wales. I met the whole band, and they were really good. I was riding back with them after the show, and the band and manager were all drinking, and at one point, I ended up being the only sober driver. Somehow, I ended up driving on the wrong side of the road in London at 3 a.m. and nearly killed everybody. I was totally sober, but it being late and driving on what was the wrong side of the road—for me—was very confusing. I am sure they remember the wild ride at the hands of the crazy American. I swore I would never drive in London again.

SC: Do you remember the name of the Level 42 album you worked on?

GS: I don't, but I do remember it was around the fall of 1981. Jet lag, big shows, travel, and all that stuff was tough. I do remember the project was with MCA, because I went into the studio with Wilton [Felder] to listen to the mix of the live show. Wilton was the producer of The Crusaders, but he would always give the rest of the band co-producer credits.

So, we were listening to the mix, and there are 48 tracks, and of those 48 tracks, they are divided into tracks dedicated solely to the orchestra, tracks for BB King and his band, and then those tracks for The Crusaders. Even further, for the drummer, there are tracks for the hi-hat, the tom-tom, and a track for the bass drum. So, we have each of the 48 tracks dedicated to one portion of what was being performed onstage.

It was a live album—we were recording the whole performance—and Wilton comes in and starts asking just to hear the guitar, or just to hear the cymbal, and he starts picking it apart with, "He is playing too fast, he is off a beat, he missed that note" and on and on and on. We spent the afternoon going over each one of these tracks, and with so much going on, if a cymbal is a half measure late or early, it is not really going to be as audible as when listening to a stripped down mix.

There is something called the monitor mix, which is the output of what I was doing, and I ran an outbound line to a cassette tape so I could keep a record and hear everything that was done. Wilton calls the manager and tells him the album sucks and it can't be released, because he is picking apart every nuance that happens with live shows. I was thinking that these five days spent on the project might not see the light of day because Wilton couldn't recognize the difference between working in the studio and working on a grand, huge-scale project. I didn't say anything, but I was concerned for sure.

From London, we went to Paris down to the Champs-Elysees, and played a beautiful little 3,000-seat theater, and the acoustics were amazing. I couldn't help but think that should have been the venue to record the live album, because the sound quality and the acoustics were marvelous. It was fabulous.

So, we were hanging out with BB, and he was telling stories about how he had just gotten back from doing a show in Russia while still under The Iron Curtain. He was one of the first bands allowed to play there, so I asked him about it, and he went on to tell this story about how he and Lucille were treated in the Soviet Union.

One story was how, after a gig, they went back to the hotel room, as they weren't allowed to do anything after shows. So, the band would sit in the hotel and play cards.

One night, it was 3 or 4 in the morning, and they were playing poker. Someone in the band mentioned off-hand how it would be great to have some coffee. The band didn't think anything of it, and kept on playing cards, but 10 minutes later, there came a knock on the door, and room service came in with a pot of coffee. They later realized their room was bugged, and everything they said was overheard.

I will never forget BB's quote: "The one thing I learned in Russia was not to talk."

I believe him, too, because BB always told the truth, and seemed like a real honest, straightforward guy.

Paris was not very nice to us. I was a white guy playing with a black group, and everything we did was first-class, but they did not treat us well. Everywhere else we traveled, we were treated great, but Paris was different. They were just rude and angry.

SC: Are you sure it was a case of racism, and not Paris being Paris? They are not a city known for their kind treatment and hospitality towards tourists and foreigners.

GS: The band certainly felt it was racist, and traveling with the band, and how we were treated in other places compared to there, I could see why they felt that way, because I felt it, too.

We would sit down at a bar, and they would serve everybody but us. We would take the train, and the porters, who were helping everyone with their bags, would walk away when it was our turn to board.

After Paris, we went to Copenhagen and Amsterdam. I remember, as we were leaving Amsterdam, I actually wrote a song called, "I Have

Never Slept in Amsterdam." It was so much fun, and there was so much going on.

It was funny, too, because, at this point of the tour, I had gotten to know the band members. Wilton would never go out, but Joe would, and Sticks would just disappear. His brother, Tom, was the road manager, so Joe, Tom, and I would all go out together.

As our shows in Europe were televised a lot of the time, people would recognize us. We would be out in a bar or a pub, and these beautiful girls would slide over to us and bring out vials of coke to share. It was a fun night there in Amsterdam, and that was the reason I wrote that song, because none of us slept at all that night.

I remember, when we were in Berlin, we were all taking a bus through Checkpoint Charlie. Some of the guys were sleeping, and I was sitting behind the bus driver. The line to get through was three or four hours long, so it was a really boring wait. We finally got to the front of the line, and the bus door opened and this guy with a machine gun came in barking orders in German.

I am sitting behind the driver, and he walks up to me, slaps my sunglasses off of my face, and looks me right in the eyes while still yelling at me in German. I have no clue what he is saying. So, he goes through the bus, checking IDs and passports, giving us impromptu interrogations. I later found out from the promoter that the guards were not looking for drugs, but were looking for people. The drugs moving through there were widespread, and the promoter said anyone in the city could get you anything you wanted.

Later that night, I went for a walk to see the Berlin Wall, and there was a bombed-out church that stood as a memorial. Standing by that church, you could feel the death and destruction in the area. It had such a weird, emotional vibe to it, where you knew the area had seen some bleak, desperate times.

It was funny, because when we went back across the border into West Berlin, the guards all spoke English, and, as opposed to being barked at and yelled at, all the guards wanted were promo records and promo stuff, and were totally nice and polite. It was such a huge difference!

SC: You mentioned you toured Japan and Asia with the band as well. What were those areas like?

GS: Japan was great.

We went for a week, and the main reason we went, was to record one of the first two-track digital recordings. Now, there were only two tracks, which meant no overdubs or advanced mixes and whatnot, but it was one of the very first digital recordings ever.

RCA Victor, as they were known in Japan, wanted to show it off by recording The Crusaders. We did the show straight, because with only two tracks, it was what it was, and I did that—just running the left/right audio lines directly from the output of the mixing board to the inputs on the recorder with no mixers or other effects at all.

What a difference it was, though, between London and Tokyo!

By the time we reached Japan, we had our routine down as to what we did when we got to the airport, where we would put all of our bags in a circle and have someone guard the bags while the other went to the bathroom, the snack shop, or wherever.

In Japan, the promoter came over to me as I guarded the bags with this puzzled look and asked, "What are you doing?"

I tell him that I'm guarding the bags, and he says, "No one steals in Japan," and looks at me like I am a complete fool for not knowing that. It was then that I realized we weren't in Europe anymore.

I loved Tokyo. The other thing I remember was staying in this place called the New Otani Hotel that was all complete first-class. We had five shows to do there, and during that time, I rode the bullet train through this huge tunnel that went under the water and the whole bit. Every time you talked to the girls there, they would blush and cover their mouths and giggle.

So, we had our meeting, and it was the 5th show that was to be recorded. We went all over Tokyo, Nagoya, and some other places. They were so well organized, though. Every show we did, the layout and the preparation from the Japanese staff was identical. They would always ask if you needed anything else, and it was amazing, because they would pinpoint the exact time they would be there to give what you wanted. If you needed a cable, they would say, "The cable will be delivered at 2:04," and—sure enough—at 2:04, here would come this guy with your cable.

We had a second meeting for one of the shows where they had an interpreter for me, since I couldn't speak Japanese, and the interpreter asked if they has missed something about me. I didn't understand what they were asking or what they wanted, and then they pulled out this book that had all of my information about anything I had ever done in my whole career. They knew stuff about me that I had forgotten for years. They knew more about me than I knew about me, and I was beginning to get worried they knew what I did in Amsterdam.

So, we went and did our setup, sound check, and whatnot; and I wanted to add some echo, so I asked, "Where is a patch cord?" and the whole room is dead silent—total silence. I ask the interpreter what the problem was, and he said I had insulted them by not asking them to do it. So, I am like, "So, not having them do my job was insulting to them?"

After that, it was fabulous! I could just bark out orders and have everything set up perfectly for me. The Japanese helping me there were like a Swiss watch or something, where they were just efficient at doing their jobs, polite and happy to help. In England, if you asked someone to do something, you'd have some drunk guy telling you to fuck off. The Japanese were still gracious enough to let me work the board, but all the wiring and setup…they took care of everything. The culture there was amazing. I loved it.

SC: How did the digital taping [sic] go?

GS: We got the concert and the whole show, but the sound quality came off as brittle. The highs were really high, but there was bottom-end loss. So, it was great to be part of that history in the making, but the quality wasn't as precise and full as you have now. That was one of the first-ever digital recordings for RCA Victor Japan, and they were using it to promote digital recording. Then, it was state-of-the-art; now, it's something any teenager can do on his computer with ProTools.

Anyhow, the Japanese executives loved the whole production of the concerts, though. One was broadcast on live Japanese TV, and it was a huge deal. The album was called "The Crusaders Live in Japan." We finished the show, got back to the hotel, and the phone rings; it is Tom, the road manager, who says the president of RCA Victor Japan was thrilled with the show and the performance, and he wanted to take the band out for the night, and—if I wanted—to go out with him, Joe, and the president. So, Joe, Tom, and I meet out in the lobby, and this limo pulls up and president of RCA Victor walks out of the limo, and he is about 4' tall.

SC: Was he bigger than David Geffen?

GS: Hah! It was pretty close!

I can tell you he was much nicer and kept repeating, "Thank you very much," all night long.

So, we got into the limo, and not much is being said. We are driving around Tokyo, and I notice we are going from the flashy, high-dollar area, to an area that is a little more low-key and almost middleclass-looking. I asked the limo driver where we were going, and he told us that this was the Tokyo version of their red-light district.

We go inside this little unassuming restaurant, where they served meat on sticks.

SC: I believe that is referred to as yakitori.

GS: That sounds right.

Anyhow, as we are sitting there eating and hanging out, the TV starts replaying our show we just did. So, we are sitting there, drinking sake and eating with the President of RCA Japan, and he looks at us and says, "You will soon be very happy."

Not a moment later, a guy comes in and points to Joe Sample, and says, "Follow me." So, Joe leaves with him. Three or four minutes later, he comes back and points to Tom and says the same thing.

Now, it's just the President and me, and I am sitting there, not knowing what to think. It seemed longer than three or four minutes when it was finally my turn, but soon, the guy comes back and tells me to follow him.

We leave the restaurant and get into this Mercedes, and we drive a little bit to this little house and the guy says, "You have present of bath house." So, I go inside this house, and it is a Japanese bathhouse. It was this room with different levels and a drain on the bottom, and this Japanese girl would bathe you and basically service you in any way you wanted. It was maybe the greatest night of my life from start to finish.

We got back to the restaurant, and Joe and Tom were all sitting at the same table grinning at me as I walked through the door. Once again, the president says, "Thank you very much," as we get back into the limo and back to the hotel.

I'll never forget it; that was the highlight of 1981 and the tour. After that, we toured the Philippines, and it was a bit different from Japan. I will always have a warm spot in my heart for Japan.

SC: Tell us about Manila. I am not sure if you are familiar with the story, but The Beatles had a bad experience in the Philippines as well.

GS: We did one show, and the only reason we stopped there was because we were going from the Philippines to Hawaii. We went to Hawaii because customs was easier in Hawaii than it was in LA, and we were bringing back all sorts of electronics from Japan.

The idea was to finish the last show in the Philippines, hang in Hawaii for a few days, and then go back to LA. I had bought one of the first Sony Walkmans in Japan, and I was using it to listen to the board mixes of the show that I had done. Sticks had thousands of dollars of electronics with him. In Hawaii, you could throw some money at the customs agent and walk through the line, but LA was different.

So, we arrive in Manila, go to customs, get all of our equipment checked in, and do the bag count to make sure we have everything. As we go through customs, they simply wave us through without stamping our passports. We just thought we were big stars or something.

We walk around the town, meet the promoter, and all that stuff. But my impression of the country, especially after visiting Tokyo, was that it was a total third-world country with poverty and all that. I used to always give my change to the kids there whenever I could, and that kind of thing. We played our show and everything, but now it was time to leave.

We get to the airport, and there were droves of peasants outside the airport trying to get in, and we were basically fighting our way through all of them. This was towards the end of the Marcos regime, so there was all this political turmoil and whatnot.

We actually got to visit the presidential palace while we were there. It was pretty impressive, and they were nice people, but it was quite the contrast to see the poverty there.

Anyhow, as we get into the airport, and we are ready to leave, the same customs agent who waved us through without stamping our passports was now telling us we couldn't leave because we didn't have a stamp. Our flight was in an hour, so Tom just started offering him money. Finally, five minutes before the flight, Tom had to pay the guy $1,000 bucks to let us go and get on the plane. It was a funky experience.

SC: Not surprised to hear that story. If The Beatles could get shaken down to leave the country, it could happen to anyone.

GS: That is exactly what it was—a shake down.

SC: You got lucky. There were a couple of guys in The Beatles' entourage who got physically attacked and roughed up, or so the story goes. Speaking of The Beatles, and now that we are into the 80s, tell us how you came to meet and work with Billy Preston.

GS: Well, that leads me back to more Crusaders stuff. We got back into town, and *Street Life* was so popular that Wilton Felder and Joe Sample were both offered solo albums. So, I started recording those projects.

SC: Did Wilton ever lighten up or loosen up with you?

GS: No, he was always tense. Wilton never lightened up, and working with him was tough, because he would layer and layer and overdub and overdub. When you are recording, the more stuff you add to a song, the less pronounced each of the individual parts is going to be within the mix.

So, we would add layer after layer, and all these overdubs, and then he would complain that I ruined the mix because the bass was no longer audible. I finally broke down and said, "Wilton, if I was to take a picture of you and you only, you would be able to see a lot of details in that picture. Now, if I was to take a picture of 30 people, and you were one of them, those details would not be as clear to see. Every time you add a layer or an overdub, you are adding more people into a group photo."

It was challenging and surprising at the same time, because he had done tons of recordings and gotten producers' credits, but the principle of wave forms and bass were concepts that he could never seem to grasp—at least, not while I was working with him.

SC: Working with Joe Sample was probably amazing by comparison.

GS: Oh yeah, Joe was easy to work with. He is a wonderful guy. He married this Swedish blonde lady who was really nice as well. Joe was just really cool and always positive, whereas it would get a little tense at times with Wilton.

At the end, we still had the BB King and The Crusaders *Royal Jam* live album from England still on the shelf. Finally, I called the manager, and hoping to get the producer's credit, and knowing it was a damned good album, called and said, "These mixes are great—Wilton is wrong. You should release these tapes. If you give me the studio and this budget, I will mix it and do everything, provided you give me a point if they decide to use it."

So, I got $25,000 to budget studio time, and was able to rework all of the mixes to be presented. It was a pain. I had to do some hand-mixing and some other things to get it sounding good, and—keep in mind—I wasn't charging my engineering time like I could have. I was going to do the engineering and mixing for free, knowing I would get it back with royalties.

Anyhow, MCA loved it, released it, and it ended up being the 2nd biggest seller for them behind *Street Life*. For all of my work, I got nothing for it. I got a call from their manager, who said Wilton wrote me out of the picture, and could not let anyone else get a producer's credit on any Crusaders record, so I got nothing.

It was their 2nd biggest selling album, and Wilton screwed me. I said "Fuck you," hung up the phone, and never worked with them again. It says on all of their records that Wilton is producer, with the exception of that album, which gives Wilton credit as Executive Producer. He knew he couldn't take any credit as the producer, so he wrote himself in as Executive Producer.

SC: Nowadays, you probably could have sued them and gotten something.

GS: Yeah, but as you know by now, that just wasn't my style. I was still doing a lot of work recording disco albums, though the scene was starting to fade out.

SC: A side question: who recorded the song, "Boogie Woogie Woogie Dancing Shoes?"

GS: That was some girl group—I think they were called A Taste of Honey. One of those singers, Hazel Payne, was married to a guy who worked at MCA. His name was Steve Buckley—he was the head of A&R for their R&B division.

SC: So, how does this end up with you meeting Billy Preston?

GS: Well, it starts with me meeting Enzo Bilinelli and Dina Al-Fassi. They were friends with my business partner at that time, Ralph Benatar. Dina was Enzo's sister, and they were from Europe—Italy or something. We used to refer to his sister as "Sheika Dina." They had made news from her then-husband, Sheik Al-Fassi, who bought this huge mansion in Beverly Hills, and he painted all sorts of crazy colors and painted pubic hair on the statues that were prominently displayed in the front. It was a big story in the 80s, and the whole place later burned to the ground. They were living in the guesthouse, as that was the only structure still standing after the fire and they wanted to be investors in one of our music projects.

We would go up to the mansion and had a mutual friend who owned a studio called "Salty Dog Studios." His name was David Coe, and I discussed finding a black artist that was down on his luck with him. I suggested Billy Preston, because when I did work for Barry Gordy at Motown, I had met his manager, Tony Jones.

Davis Coe gave Tony Jones a call, and set up a meeting at Salty Dog Studios. We discussed producing an album for Billy, but Tony decided to have us first finish an album that was incomplete for Motown called *Pressin' On*. That was his final album for Motown, so we then signed Billy to our production company, Sheika Productions. We later formed a corporation with Billy, called P.S.B.B. Inc. The company managed and produced one album with Billy Preston, named *On The Air*.

Billy was a frequent visitor to the guesthouse at the mansion because it was known as a "party house," and always had something going on. He was in between careers—I guess you could say—and that's to put it politely.

This photo was taken at the Sheik Al-Fasi mansion on Sunset Blvd. in the early 80's, the mansion with painted pubic hair statues. From left to right, Ralph Benatar, unknown, Billy Preston, Enzo Bilinelli, and Galen Senogles.

So, since we now had investors with Enzo, Sheika Dina, and the guy with Salty Dog Studios, and along with my musical pedigree, the idea was that we would revitalize Billy's career by managing and producing him.

I sold Billy on the idea, and Enzo and Sheika Dina as well, because they loved the idea of working with and being part of The Fifth Beatle's career and all that. I will say this about Billy: he was a talented, talented man. I was able to get the project started by giving

Billy a salary, and at this time, he was behind on rent, had bills, and was pretty much in financial ruin.

Now, all of Billy's big hits, like, "Nothing From Nothing" and "That's The Way God Planned It" were all on A&M with Herb Albert and Jerry Moss. So, we went to A&M first to see if they would be interested in the project. We set up a meeting with their attorneys and our attorneys, Billy, Jerry Moss, and myself.

It was going great, and I was thinking we were going to get a deal from A&M. We were going to play the demos, but Jerry Moss says he does not even need to hear them, and just wanted to talk with Billy. He starts by asking Billy about the ranch that Billy owned in Topanga, and some other personal details about Billy's life. After about 15 minutes, he says, "Sorry Billy, you haven't changed, and we can't work with you—pass."

He hadn't changed at all, and was still doing a lot of drugs, and Jerry Moss knew it. The meeting got pretty cold after that. I suppose looking back, credit Jerry Moss for being smart enough to see the risk factors involved with signing Billy at that time.

SC: Billy had a lot of personal issues–some proven, and some just rumored. Working with him, side-by-side, what was really going on with Billy at that time?

GS: The truth was that, not only did Billy have a serious drug problem, but he also liked the services of young men…and in some cases, young boys.

One of these young men that Billy was seeing at the time happened to be Mark Davis, son of Sammy Davis, Jr. I actually met Sammy a few times, but that is a story for another time.

Anyhow, I remember one day I went to visit Sheika Dina's on Sunset Blvd. As I mentioned, at this time, the mansion had burned down, but they were living in the guesthouse. I arrive, and there is famous divorce attorney Marvin Michelson, Sheika Dina, Billy, and Mark Davis, and they are all sitting around doing coke in the front room of the guest house.

So, I sit down, they hand me the mirror, and I do some. It was funny, because, once again, here I am, this kid from Kansas, doing coke with the most famous lawyer in the world at that time, his client that had made millions from the divorce settlement—Billy Preston—and Sammy Davis Jr.'s son, who may have still been a teenager at that time.

SC: Were Billy and Mark Davis a couple at that time?

GS: Yeah, I think they were and I think Mark was only 16 or 17 at that time, too.

So, all of a sudden, we hear a car coming up the drive, and we hear the car stop. We look outside to see who it is, and out from the car steps Sammy Davis Jr....and he is holding a handgun.

He slams the car door and starts yelling, "Where is Billy? Where is Billy?" Billy runs out of the house, and Sammy points the gun at him, aims the gun with his good eye at Billy's head, and says, "If you ever touch my son again I will shoot your nigger ass, you motherfucker." Billy starts running, and Sammy starts chasing him.

SC: Let me get this straight: Sammy Davis Jr., gun in hand, is chasing Billy Preston down Sunset Blvd.?

GS: Exactly. They ended up down at Will Rogers Park over by the Beverly Hills Hotel, and as I was catching up to them, I could hear someone yelling, "Don't kill him! Don't kill him!"

By the time I got there, they must have worked it out. I can tell you I never saw Billy with Mark Davis again. I thought for sure that Sammy was going to kill him, because he had all of the resources and power where he could have gotten away with it.

SC: That is the most amazing story I have ever heard....maybe the best celebrity story few people have ever heard.

GS: It was one of those stories you certainly could not have made up, but it happened—I was there to see it firsthand.

SC: You and Marvin Michelson.

GS: Yeah, it was the 80s in Los Angeles—for better or worse.

SC: At that time, was Billy doing cocaine every day?

GS: He never did it around me when we were doing business or had things to take care of, but I knew he was doing it. He was good about hiding it, and could be sneaky. I managed him for a while after we did the record and did shows in Vegas and everything. He was usually unreachable while we were in Vegas, but to his credit, when he had a show, he would get there just in time and put on a great performance. He was one of those guys who would show up completely loaded, but still be a total professional when it was show time. He could handle himself. Be it a concert or an interview, he could be totally loaded, but pull it together when it was needed.

We were playing The Sahara in Vegas when I was managing him, and he had a gig there where we were making $10,000 a week. The boss at The Sahara was a guy named Rudy Garino. He had this crooked nose and gravelly voice, and he would call me when it was time to get paid.

In true Vegas Casino style, he'd asked for me to meet him behind the dollar slot machines. He would give me a stack of hundreds, and I would ask, "Do you want me to sign something?" and he would just say, "Nah, you know I paid ya."

SC: So it was like getting paid by the mob?

GS: It certainly felt that way. I would go to deposit the money, and some of the bills ended up being counterfeit. I asked the bank teller at home if I would get reimbursed, and he said I had to turn them in, but I kept the bills instead. I later managed to pass the counterfeit money back to The Sahara by simply using those same bills to spend at the restaurants and the bars.

SC: So, those counterfeit bills were almost like accepted currency at The Sahara.

GS: They probably were. Every week, I would go meet Rudy behind the dollar slots to get paid. We would take our cut for managing him, and used the rest to pay some of Billy's debts. At the end of the day, we probably paid a quarter of a million for Billy, trying to get things worked out and get him back on track.

We were able to cut the album, and we had an attorney. We were also able to find a small label in San Francisco—because we had played there a couple of times—and the owners of this label liked Billy.

BEATLE TRIBUTE

WORDS AND MUSIC BY
BILLY PRESTON
RALPH BENATAR
GALEN SENOGLES
JOHN LENNON
PAUL McCARTNEY

© 1984, IRVING MUSIC, INC. AND WEP MUSIC AND SIMPLE SONG MUSIC (BMI)
AND NORTHERN SONGS LTD.
ALL RIGHTS RESERVED INT'L. COPYRIGHT SECURED

JUDY GREEN MUSIC

At that time, a lot of it had to do with Billy being gay, and they were gay, so they had some things in common, which made it seem like it was going to be a good fit. I later came to find out that our attorney happened to also be their attorney as well, which became a huge conflict of interest.

This ended up being catastrophic for us, because the owner of this small label ended up dying of AIDS, and once he died, and due to the fact our lawyer was also their lawyer, it basically meant we weren't going to get paid what we were owed for sales of the record.

Bottom line: they owed us $50,000 that just disappeared. That was the album, *On the Air*, in which I co-wrote a couple of songs with Billy, including the one called, "Beatle Tribute."

SC: Now, you have been screwed over for your engineer credit on Pink Floyd's *The Wall*, an engineering credit on *Rumours*, screwed over by The Crusaders for the producer credit on the *Royal Jam* album, and then screwed over again on the Billy Preston album for payment; was this why you decided to leave the music business?

GS: It certainly played a part in making my decision, for sure. There were some other things that happened after that, as well, that also contributed that we can talk about, but I am no fan of the music industry, and now, with digital downloading and pirating being so easy, I really have no sympathy for anyone in the industry.

SC: You had a foray into soul and black music, right?

GS: Right around '84 and '85, I was able to transition into those genres, and it proved to be the final straw for my music career.

Because of the work I had done with The Crusaders, and, to some extent, working with Billy, I already had what I guess they call "street cred" now, so I was able to keep working. I did a lot of work with the DeBarge family: El, Chico, Bunny, James, and all of them.

SC: At the time, they were trying to position the DeBarge family as the next Jackson family, weren't they?

GS: That's right.

There was a lot of buzz and hype and all that stuff, and I did almost all of their records. So, at that time, I decided I was going to go ahead and build my own studio. I didn't have a lot of resources, but had enough to turn my garage into a fully functional recording studio.

I had one of the first MIDI rooms* in Los Angeles. I had a 48-track recording system, and later, I was one of the first rooms to transition into all-digital recording. I became a beta tester for the early version of ProTools and Apple. We had drum machines, synths—all of it. I was one of the first studios to fully embrace that aspect of digital recording.

So, I met the DeBarges, and did records for Chico and James. I met them through Billy Preston because, well, all of the DeBarges at the time were teenage boys. Billy had set up a small demo studio in his house that we put in for him. We bought all the equipment and set it up, so Billy was recording, or (supposedly), having the DeBarges over to record demos at his house.

I remember we were doing some work with them when James DeBarge was married to Janet Jackson. Once that marriage got annulled, James was specifically thinking Michael Jackson was against the marriage and was behind the annulment. James came into the studio, and you could see that he was livid. He was yelling, "I am going to tell the world about what Michael is doing to those young boys up in his room."

* Note-MIDI is an electronic musical instrument industry specification that enables a wide variety of digital musical instruments, computers, and other related devices to connect and communicate with one another. It marked the advent of the modern age of digital recording commonly used today.

SC: So, he was claiming that Michael Jackson was molesting children, and he was going to go to the press?

GS: Correct. He said he was going to come out and tell the world about Michael Jackson. Somehow, that all got calmed down, and I never heard about it again.

I was making a lot of money at the time with the studio, and doing work with DeBarge and other black-oriented pop music. Eventually, I got signed to a big deal with Warner Brothers, and spent $200,000 updating my studio in North Hollywood to a complete studio with a live room and the whole bit.

One story I remember about that studio and El DeBarge was in the early 90s, and what was happening with the LA Riots. Anyone in or near Los Angeles was nervous about what was going on. I think I had it on the TV or something, and El came in and said, "Don't worry, man. I just talked with Farrakhan, and here it is." He took a piece of paper, wrote something on it, and told me to put it in the window. If I did that, the building wouldn't get burned and looted.

I asked him, "Farrakhan?"

El said, "Yeah, he is running the whole show, and as long as you keep that paper in the window, you will be alright."

So, based on what El DeBarge told me that night, I always was of the mind that Louis Farrakhan was the mastermind behind the LA Riots.

SC: What was it he wrote on the paper that was in the window?

GS: I don't remember at all, but I wish I did. El was completely serious and calm about the whole thing. Judging by his demeanor, I think he was telling the truth—or at least believed that was the truth. I believed him. Why wouldn't I? El was well-connected with LA's black community.

SC: Did any other places near you get hit during the riot?

GS: None on my block, fortunately, but I had some friends who had a studio on Beverly and Fairfax over by CBS and the Farmers Market called Cherokee Studios. I was a friend of the Robb brothers, who had built it and worked there, and we were industry friends. They had some hits in the Sixties and at that time, Cherokee was one of the hotter studios to record in.

After the riot was over, one of the Robb's called me up and asked if my studio survived the riot. I told him everything was okay, and asked how his studio was. He then told me this story about how they had boarded up all of the windows in the studio, and because their building was an industrial-type building, it had the flat roof and a small wall running around the perimeter of the building.

They had gotten some guns and bullets to protect the studio—like some of the Korean store owners had done during the riots. They were standing on the roof and watched as a big SUV pulled up to the Radio Shack across the street, and four gang members got out and threw a brick in the window and looted the place. When they were done, they started heading across the street to the studio and tried to take the boards off the building, when the owners fired a few warning shots. Next thing they know, a full Wild West-style gunfight ensues, with the owners and the gang members exchanging rounds.

The gang members got back into the SUV and left. Thirty minutes later, an LAPD car pulls up on Fairfax. They flagged the cops down and told them the story about the shootout with the gang members. The cops gets out of their car and walk to the back, open the trunk, hand them some more ammunition, and then tell them that they are on their own and wished them good luck. They got back into their patrol car and left.

SC: I heard similar stories, so that does not surprise me at all. The El Debarge/Farrakhan connection, however, is one that will probably draw some attention—not to mention the Michael Jackson hearsay.

GS: Like I said, these were all things that I vividly remember. It was years ago, so I have probably forgotten a ton of stories as well, but those stories I remember specifically like it was yesterday.

SC: You were telling me that you spent some time in the Playboy Mansion and had some interaction with Hugh Hefner?

GS: This was 1984, and had to do with my wife and my Porsche.

It was New Years' Eve, and my wife was a former centerfold. She knew a lot of people involved with Playboy Magazine, so we would spend New Years' Eve and their Mid-Summer August party there at the Playboy Mansion.

The story starts back when we were touring Germany with The Crusaders, though. As I was in Germany around 1983, I went to Stuttgart, as I was involved with something called the Porsche Owner's

Club, and as part of the club, you would take your car to these tracks and race your 911.

That year, I was named Rookie of the Year of the Porsche Owner's Club, and still have a trophy to prove it. I got the day off from the tour with The Crusaders, and was able to visit the Porsche factory. When I was touring the factory, one of the staff there asked if I wanted to drive the new 944 on the Autobahn.

The 944, was brand new, and I was doing 120mph and loving it. The guys at the factory tell me it's going to be released soon and asked if I wanted one. I loved it and had one ordered and shipped back to the States. It arrived in September or October of that year, and I drove it to the Playboy Mansion on New Years' Eve.

This was one of the first cars in the US that had an Unger Car alarm. There was a five-digit code you had to enter to keep the engine running. It was called an "Unger" alarm, which meant that, unless you entered the code, the car would still run for 30 seconds or something before shutting down.

In those days, you would drive into the Mansion and park at the fountain, where a valet would then park your car; now, they have you park down the hill and bus you into the Mansion, and that is probably my fault as a result of this story.

I drive to the fountain, and give the valet the story about the code. They write "alarm" on the valet ticket, and I then go on into the Mansion for the New Years Eve party.

So, I leave the party around 2 or 3 in the morning, and we are all a bit tipsy with champagne, girls, and all the stuff that happens at the Playboy parties. I come to the fountain, and I see my car with smoke coming from the hood. I had been drinking, so the valet gets us into the car and pushes it down the hill to the gate.

The car won't go into gear, the transmission is gone, I am pissed off and sobering up because my new car won't drive. I walk back up to the top of the hill, back to the fountain in the driveway to meet the head of security, whose name was Joe.

I'm furious. Joe calms me down, brings out a hundred dollar bottle of champagne, and ensures us that they will cover all the costs and whatnot, and get us a ride home.

We go back into the house, go to the sun-tanning room, and some guy there starts hitting on my wife. At the Playboy Mansion, anything goes; but the cardinal rule is that if the woman says no, then she is off limits.

This guy keeps trying to pick up on my wife, so I tell him I am in a horrible mood because my Porsche has just been wrecked, and if he says one more thing, I am going to deck him. He decides to says one more thing, and I start throwing punches at him. Next thing I know all hell is breaking loose.

Security comes onto the scene and breaks it up, and ends up throwing that guy out of the Mansion. They also bring me another hundred-dollar bottle of champagne.

Later, I found out that the valets would park the cars around the neighborhood and around the house, and my car happened to be parked under Hef's window. Because I had an alarm, it went off and Hef got pissed, and told the valets to shut it off. They went under the hood and ripped out a bunch of the wires and tried to go park my beautiful new Porsche in the neighborhood, but because of the shut-off feature, they had to keep jump-starting the car, and it ended up burning up the clutch.

Keep in mind, I am certified from Porsche and have awards and all this stuff directly from them, but three days later, the engine blows a rod and is done because of the parking incident. Then, they tried to blame the blown engine on me, saying it was driver error.

I had to call my lawyer, and they said I should sue the valet company, as well as Hugh Hefner. So, I had a lawsuit against both of them. Then, they said it was a defective engine, which the guys at Porsche did not like at all.

Finally, nine months later, my day in court comes up, and that morning, I get a phone call from my lawyer, who tells me the president of Porsche is on the line and wants to talk with me. I get on the phone, and the president says they are going to pay to have my engine replaced. I told him, "This wasn't your fault. It was the valets' fault and lets go after them."

He then says that, on advice from his attorney, Porsche was just going to pay for everything because they could not afford to take the chance.

So, just like that, they covered all of the bills for the car I was leasing and all of the repairs. After that, the people working at the Mansion never let anyone drive there again, and started bussing people in from UCLA.

SC: You mentioned you had more than one encounter with Sammy Davis Jr.

GS: Shortly after the Porsche incident, I was invited to Sammy's house. It was a really nice house, and he actually owned one pair of the ruby slippers from The Wizard of Oz. He had all kinds of stuff there, it was almost like a museum.

Anyhow, we were sitting there, and I told Sammy the story about the Porsche and Sammy said, "I would have taken that car to Hugh's bedroom and told him to get fucked. That's the way we did it." Even in his off time, he was full-blown Rat Pack.

SC: So, after the DeBarges, what happened with your music career?

GS: I was doing all sorts of work for Motown. That's who was handling them at the time, and I spent some time with Berry Gordy.

Motown was just starting to get involved with rap. The first rap artist they sent me was this huge guy who had to have been 350 pounds, and the first thing he did was sit down next to me, pull out a Glock that he set on the control board, and said, "The music business ain't like the music business used to be."

That was my first taste of working with rap artists. I did a few projects here and there, and one with Snoop Dogg, who came in with El DeBarge one time. No one had heard of him at that time, and someone in their crew ended up stealing some guitars and mics. They knew what they were doing, too, because they were stealing the good, high-end stuff.

SC: Snoop stole some of your equipment?

GS: Him or someone with him. A couple of weeks later, I got a call from the North Hollywood PD, who sent me a warning about a rap group who had a white female manager booking late studio time. They would come in, bound and gag the owner, and then ransack the studio for all of the equipment. It had already happened with two other studio owners, and after my experiences with the fat guy and the Glock, and Snoop stealing my Stratocaster, I had just about had enough of the music business.

What happened from the 80s on, was that the importance of sound quality diminished, and I was a sound guy. In the 70s, it was all about how good could you make the sound which totally appealed to me and was right up my alley. It was a natural fit. But in the 80s and 90s, with rap music and rap groups, it was all about how shitty you could make it sound, and how cheaply you could do it. When some guy was able to record something for $500 bucks, the music companies were all over it—they loved it.

I did a record with Joe Cooley called, *Fuck New York* that was a big hit that I gave them free studio time for. They didn't give back, say thanks, or anything. They called it California Rap, which I shortened to C-RAP, which I shortened, again, to just "crap." It was the end of my interest in the music business, and after that, I got into doing sound for some well known blockbuster movies you have probably heard of, but that's another story altogether.

SC: In the last couple of chapters, we heard the story about how you became a musician, ended up in the business, and subsequently why you left the music business. I want to get a bit deeper into certain subjects we briefly covered.

You were involved with recording some of the most famous rock albums of all time, and a big part of those albums' enduring popularity stems from the sound quality. Like on Steely Dan's *Aja*, [The Beatles'] *Abbey Road* or [Pink Floyd's] *Dark Side of The Moon*…even if you don't know a song, you can still listen to it on the radio and go, "Man, that's a very clean sound!" You can hear every instrument—bass, organ...the separation of each individual instrument is amazing! So, what is it they do in the studio to bring out that clarity and that separation?

GS: The first thing they do is pick the right studio.

SC: [laughs]

GS: I'm serious. Each studio back then had its own characteristics and sound. Producer's Workshop had that type of sound, plus, what it was really noted for, was its bottom-en and by bottom-end, I mean the sound of the kick drum, the sound of the bass, the lower frequencies.

SC: So, The Producer's Workshop was known for being able to get the low lows?

GS: That's the most difficult thing to record.

It was the studio itself...when you walked into it, it looked like The Crab Shack compared to a super-fancy five-star restaurant. It was all about the sound—the whole thing was about sound. It wasn't like The Record Plant, where they had a Jacuzzi, the girls, and all that stuff.

It was on Hollywood Blvd. behind The Mastering Lab.

SC: Okay, so, The Producer's Workshop was known for the low-end, and being able to get the lower drums and those things. What was Sunset Sound like? What was their claim to fame, as far as audio quality?

GS: They had bigger rooms, and their sound was kind of more like a live room. They had a more crisp sound, actually. It would draw people in who had a bigger entourage. Their quality was...good...but it was more "good enough." That was where we did Ringo's *Goodnight, Vienna*, but Producer's Workshop...It was hand-built by Bud Wyatt, and Bill Schnee came there to work as well, and he was one of the greatest engineers of the era. He knew it sounded so good…Just to give a little idea—then we're going to go into the whole recording process—of how detailed this was for sound.

In this studio, just think of it at home, where you have your stereo on, you have your volume knob, and you turn it up and down. Well, that's called the master fader. Have you noticed that, with cheaper equipment—and I'm sure you have—the first thing to go when you turn the volume up is a sound like whissssh, wissssh [static].

SC: Yeah, yeah.

GS: That's because it gets dirty. That [knob]—it's called a pot [potentiometer]—is just a resistor that you use to turn the volume up and down. Well, what this guy did when he needed one, he didn't just buy one—he made it. They took all these different things—

SC: Bud Wyatt made it?

GS: Yeah, Bud Wyatt. I'm not an electrician, but they made their own—put little resistors on there, and they tuned them in clicks, so there would be perfect sound going through. Because, when you're recording, the last thing you hear before you hear it in the speakers is from the volume knob. If you've got a little bit of loss from something in the sound board in there, and you're not hearing it, you as an engineer wouldn't know what to compensate for, because you would never hear it in the first place. You can't adjust what you can't hear.

So, not only did they put in little resistors and built a knob, and perfectly balance everything left and right, but they'd take the resistors, and if it wasn't an exact ohm, they would take a razor blade and shave off part of it! These guys were nuts, right?

So, the place had this sound, so the people that went there—like Richard Perry and Bill Schnee, and all those people we talked about—made a name for it, and all these groups that came in like Fleetwood Mac and Steely Dan knew it.

You once asked me a question about Steely Dan. Well, Donald Fagan went there specifically because of that sound—and to be more specific—the cleanliness of the sound.

He could get that drum sound you're talking about. He could get that clean bass, he could get the guitar…

One of the hardest things to record back then—and he used it a lot—was the Fender Rhodes piano. That was a cool piano sound. They are hard to record, because they distort really easily, and they're not clean, so when you're talking—

SC: Like when you're playing that live, it sounds brilliant, but it's hard to get that same tonal quality…

GS: Correct. At times, the same levels in a live setting become completely distorted in the studio. So, when I talk loud into a mic on stage, it may sound great, but when that same mic and those same settings were used in the studio, you would need to spend all of this time making all the adjustments to get those same tones and audio properties. Because of the electronics in the studio, that, in essence, became the value of good production.

SC: Okay. What made some studios preferable to others?

GS: It was a choice, you know. Like, in some studios—like the Record Plant—they were rock 'n roll. They were able to get a good guitar sound. For whatever reason, they were able to add a little dirt to it.

SC: Dirt?

GS: We called it dirt, or grime, or distortion.

Some rock 'n roll bands would go over there—and it wasn't just because of the Jacuzzi or the girls and that they could party. The guitars sounded better. Guitar groups, when they'd come in and would go to Producer's Workshop, would go, "Ahh, no! That's too clean! I got to have a little more grunge or distortion. This doesn't work!"

Another thing I'm going to get into later when we get really deep into recording: I'm going to go through how we recorded David Gilmour's guitar solo on "Another Brick In The Wall", which is arguably one of the most famous solos of all time.

SC: Sure—that, and "Comfortably Numb."

GS: Later on, I'm going to tell you a little story about "Comfortably Numb" as well.

SC: Now, you mentioned that some studios, like The Record Plant, had a better sound for guitar bands. In those days, too, the guys said they would go to The Producer's Workshop and it was too clean for them. But, back then, it wasn't like now, where you could digitize and create any sound you wanted, right?

One other question: did you ever get to go to the Abbey Road studio in London, and look at that?

GS: I didn't go to Abbey Road, but that's funny you should ask that question. I got to go to London when I was doing disco, and there was this group, St. Tropez, which was a big dance group back then.

Well, I was working with two producers—Lauren and Rinder. We had a couple of dance hits in the late 70's.

SC: What was the big St. Tropez hit?

GS: Older songs like "Je Taime," "Belle De Jour," and "Take The 'A' Train."

SC: Okay.

GS: Songs like that, anyhow.

SC: So, they took old songs, and "disco-fied" them?

GS: They made great arrangements and elaborate horn sections. I got the album—really cool album, too.

We got to go down to Florida to do an album there, and then we went to London. When I went to London, we worked in the same studio that Elton John did all his stuff in—not Abbey Road. We have to Google the name of the studio. It was famous for Nigel Olson's drum sounds, and also they had a Trident Board, which was an English board famous for its sound.

SC: Is this was where Elton John did *Tumbleweed Connection*?

GS: I think that sounds right.

So, we were just talking about how different studios were known for different sounds. This one (in London) was known for their drum sounds, so we booked it, and they called this the "Elton John drum sound," made famous by Olson.

SC: Really? I didn't know that.

GS: His tom sounds, specifically.

SC: Oh, you mean famous with people in the music industry?

GS: Correct. Your Average Joe in the public has probably never heard of it, but for those of us in the music industry, it was common knowledge.

SC: Your casual listener wouldn't know what made it sound so good.

GS: They [the public] knew Elton John for melodies.

SC: They knew him for his piano playing, his voice and what not.

GS: I love Elton John, by the way.

SC: I agree, and I'm totally with you on that.

GS: I didn't go to Abbey Road, though.

SC: You mentioned how different studios had their own nuances and were known for being able to get good sounds for vocals, guitar, drums, and so on. In your opinion, what makes a great song, in conjunction with a great sound? We talked a little bit about how Creedence Clearwater's "Suzy Q" has such a distinct sound to it, so we can use that as an example.

GS: In my opinion, it starts with a band that has a distinct sound. Then, being able to capture that sound and that energy, and get that sound and energy of the band transferred onto tape.

With Creedence, they were able to get their sound onto the tape without losing anything, which, when it happens, is magic. What happens sometimes, though, is that some bands are far more studio-oriented than live, and they know how to maximize the options to get a specific sound.

Steely Dan, without question, is probably the best example of that.

Toto is another great example. Toto was a band formed completely from studio musicians, so it made sense that they were going to have far more experience being able to get a distinct sound onto tape that would set them apart from some garage band, or some band known for great live performances, for instance.

In this case, the studio became part of their sound and identity. Take The Rolling Stones: they were one of the first—if not the first—

to rent a house in France or somewhere, and build the studio right into the house.

SC: That was how The Stones recorded *Exile on Main Street*, right?

GS: That's right. They built the studio around the band, which gave them distinct advantages sound-wise. Back to the topic at hand; what makes a great sound has some variables.

In the 70's, sound was important, and not just for rock—it was important to have a great sound with disco, as well. With disco, they had horns, percussion, and all sorts of unique instruments they would use to boost and enhance the sound.

Not to beat a dead horse, but I got out of the business once rap started happening because artists and record companies started taking pride in making recordings as cheaply as possible. When you could record a whole album for $1,000 bucks or something, and be able to get it to chart, I knew my days were numbered, and it was the end of an era.

The music industry was almost gloating that some shitty sounding record made for nothing made the charts. To the record companies, it was all profit. Why pay for something that sounded good and was quality when a piece of shit would chart just the same?

SC: It hasn't changed, has it?

GS: I don't think it has. One thing that is a constant—no matter the studio or the sound—is the process of actually recording.

In the 70's, you had two parts of the studio: you had the control room, where the producer and engineers sat; and what we referred to as the live room. That's where the band set up with the drums, pianos, an isolated vocal booth, and whatnot. Those were the two basic parts of the studio.

You would bring your band into the studio, they would set up, and there would be a huge piece of glass that separated the band from the booth. We would call it "looking into the fishbowl." As the producer and engineer, you wanted *total control* of everything, and so you didn't want the band in on discussions and the decision-making process at all.

SC: Earlier, you had mentioned how the engineer could use the headphone volume to get a musician to play louder or softer. Was this part of the total control?

GS: That's right. We did not want some guitar player or bass player to know too much. Our job was to get that specific part and get it right—the musicians' opinions or studio knowledge was unnecessary, and, at times, could be counter-productive. Hence, we had the glass, the isolation, and the complete separation.

So, you would have drums, guitars, keyboards, piano, and whatnot.

We would always record the drummer first, just because it was the loudest instrument. We would set the drums up, and depending on what studio you were at, we would do what was known as "baffling," which meant we would set up a plastic shield to block the sound of the drums.

Sometimes, we had these huge Styrofoam blocks we could use as well. You had to try to contain the drum sound, because, as the loudest instrument, it was the most likely to be picked up on other mics. It was what we called "bleed over." Then, we would set up the bass player.

In the studio, a bass player didn't need to have some huge Marshall stack or something. They would have just a simple small- or medium-sized amp.

SC: So, the bass player would bring in like a 50 watt amp, and you would just mic it to get the right sound?

GS: Typically, most bass players had their own small recording amp—usually some 15-inch speaker model. The Fender Bassman was probably the most common model you would see, and it did have a great sound. We used a method called "direct line" on about 75-80% percent of the bass tracks, where we would run one line directly into the board, and the other line to the mic in front of the amp. With two bass tracks, we could blend each track to get the best sound. By using the clean portion overdubbing the mic'd portion, you could really pull out some amazing bass sounds with great tone.

You couldn't do it with guitar, though, as that method generally ended up being far too clean of a sound. What was funny in this case is that it was always the guitar player who complained about it. They always wanted some sound that mimicked a Fender through a Vox, or a Gibson through a stack, or whatever. So, with the guitarists, we would generally be using the track from the amp, because it would give you the distortion and fuzz or whatever sound we were shooting for.

Then, the keyboard player came in. Most studios would have a piano already, so most keyboard players would bring in their electric organ, and at the time, it was typically a Fender Rhodes that we would mic direct.

At Producer's Workshop, we actually had Liberace's piano that was this 11- or 12-foot Baldwin. It was really cool. Anyhow, with pianos you would use two mics: one for the low end, and one for the high end, which you could pan to stereo with highs on the left and the lower register on the right. It would allow you to do some cool things with the highs that wouldn't apply to the lows that would give some great sounding effects.

Sometimes they wouldn't care, and they would put both mics in the middle of the piano, which was basically mono. In the studio—probably 75% of the time—all we were trying to record was spent recording the drums. Once you had the beat and the structure correct, the rest was kind of like filling in the blanks. Once you had a drum track, you could just say to Klaus Voorman, "Get back in there."

With other instruments, you can do overdubs and all sorts of tweaks through amps and effects, the control board, and tweaking the mic placement in front of the amps. With the drums, overdubbing and punching in was much harder to do.

SC: So, when you were recording the drums, was there a guide track with guitar the drummer would follow so he knew the changes?

GS: The whole band would be there playing the song, but getting the drum track first was critical to having a good session. Not all of the time—but most of the time—you had to get that drum sound.

The one time in which we got it all right from the first take was on "Mockingbird," but those are few and far between. Once again, you can change parts of guitar, bass, and vocals, but back then, the drums were live and labor-intensive.

SC: So, if you needed to get a guitar part re-recorded, it was easy to simply record the four bars needed, but with the drummer, if it was a tom fill that needed to get re-recorded, it was tricky?

GS: Oh yeah! If there were multiple parts of the drum track that needed work, it could bring the whole recording pace to a crawl. Back then, there were no click tracks or anything like that, so it all had to be done live and on the fly. Without the rest of the band to follow that segment, it took a really good drummer to be able to make those edits, and your drummer would typically play it too fast or too slow.

So, the focus was always to get the drum track first. Of course, if you were working with Richard Perry, he would replace every single track except the drums. Then, you would go into overdub mode, and with guys like Klaus Voorman, Nicky Hopkins, and Jim Keltner; they could all go in and just knock it out. That is what made them pros. With musicians who were at that level, overdubbing could be almost as time-consuming as getting a drum track.

The vocals would come next. You would start with a working mix, with just a simple guide track, and once the rest was done, the singer could come in and really give their best. With Richard Perry, he would listen and say, "Klaus, I think you could do that line better," or something like that. He would go in and replace the parts the producer thought could have been better.

I remember with Robbie Robertson, though, Richard Perry just let him do two or three takes, and he would just keep them all and listen to them later to decide which one he wanted to use and piece together. That whole process was known as "tracking"—getting each individual track down and completed. Once that was done, you could do more overdubs, bring in someone to play a conga or percussion, get some guy to play a horn, or something.

This was the beginning of the synthesizer era, so, occasionally, some studio may have a Moog or something. But in my experience, getting that solid initial drum track was key to getting a good song.

SC: How was a typical drum set mic'd up for the recording process?

GS: Well, let's use Jim Keltner's setup for example—and I use Keltner because he was the king of all studio drummers. Once again, if you could play like he played while being on acid, you are the man.

Some bigger groups would have their unique setup, but for your typical setup, for a normal group, there was the kick drum (bass drum), the snare, high hat, two shell toms, and two cymbals—one ride and one crash. That would be your set up.

I was known for my drum sound because I learned from Bill Schnee, who as I said many, many times, was maybe the best in the business.

Basically, you put a mic inside the kick drum. To get the solid sound, you would stuff pillows or blankets into the kick drum to "deaden" the sound. We found the best mic to use to capture that bottom-end that the kick drum made, and that was a real low-pressure type, loud booming sound. It wasn't easy to reproduce, but we found that a Sennheiser 421 dynamic mic was the best at capturing those low tones and bottom-end the kick drum produced.

SC: Can you talk a little bit about how you would use different mics to get different sounds, and maybe even just go into a little 70's-era Microphone 101 for studio recording?

GS: Back then, and it may be different now with the digital stuff, but there were three types of mic used in the studio.

In the case of Sennheiser, that was a dynamic mic. Dynamic mics didn't need a power source; they simply plugged in to the in jack, or input, and were able to pick up whatever was in range. When you see live shows, Shure microphones are very popular for singers, and Shure mics are generally dynamic mics.

Then, you go to FET, or transistor-powered mics, which meant that, to run the mic, you needed to have some type of power source to get it to work. The sensitivity on a FET mic was far greater than a dynamic mic, so there was no way you could use it for a kick drum.

The last type of mics we used was ribbon mics. They were the first type of microphone invented, with a big bulky square head and metal grill around it.

SC: Like the ones you see old clips of Elvis and other 50's stars singing into?

GS: Exactly. You can go back even further to the 30's and 40's and the beginning of the electronic age of amplification. Those were all ribbon mics in those days, because there were no other options. RCA, I think, were the first to manufacture it. They were really primitive, but the beauty of a ribbon mic was it would never distort. You could scream into it, or play some obnoxiously loud noise, and it was able to replicate that sound, no matter how loud, and retain the audio qualities of that sound.

Ribbon mics were great for horns and, in particular, trumpets. A trumpet is a powerful blast of audio, and ribbon mics were able to capture that tone and power.

Back to the drums, though…we always used the Sennheiser for the kick drum. Then, for the snare, you had a couple of choices. You could mic it from the top or the bottom, or—in the case of Fleetwood Mac—they would always use both, and then, during the mix, you could adjust the rattle and the pop to get a great sound coming from the snare.

Then, you would mic each individual tom. After that, you would set up what was known as a stereo overhead for the cymbals. Once that was done, each mic would then run into the console, with the bass, the snare, and each individual mic going to its own channel on the console.

What I would do—and this was taught to me by Bill Schnee—was to run the stereo track on the opposite sides of the drummer. So, if you were looking at the drummer, we would feed the right side of the drum kit to the left channel, and the left channel of the drum kit to the right channel. For the drummers' headphone mic, they would always complain, because when they listened to it, the rights were lefts and the lefts were rights—it was completely inverted. But, that's what you had to do to not only get the best sound, but also to keep track of the signals and all of that. If you tried to give a drummer a "live" mix or something, it got way too complicated and nutty. So, kick, snare, toms, cymbals, and so on…that would generally take seven or eight channels in the console to get a good, solid drum mix.

SC: Did a big name drummer in the studio inspect the drum set and the mics in the studio before recording? Did a big name care about the drum setup, or would they generally trust the engineer when it came to mic'ing up a drum set?

GS: In the case of Mick Fleetwood, he absolutely would inspect the setup. He had a lot of opinions on how the setup should be done and the way he wanted it—and you would work with them to tweak it out and set it up. That would be the starting point, but the real test came once you started recording and what it actually sounded like.

Generally, what would happen is you would spend half a day just getting the drums mic'd and ready for recording, and working it all out. Normally, what I would do is let the drummer work out some ideas: "Can I try this?" and "Can we try that?" and you would do everything you could to help the drummer get the sound that they wanted. With drummers, most of them didn't care how you got the sound as long as you got it. If you could match up the sound they wanted and get it on tape, they were happy.

SC: Was there a song from *Rumours* that you recall, when Mick Fleetwood was especially happy with the drum track you were able to capture?

GS: In the case of *Rumours*, I wasn't there to record the actual drum track—I was there for the mix—but got involved in the discussions during the mix where we were trying this and that for a specific track when they were having issues with the mix. The bass and guitar mixes were all pretty much done, and they were happy with it.

Once again, you would have a console with tape all over it, marking what track was what instrument, the backup vocals, or whatever track that was going into that specific channel of the mixing board.

One little trick I learned and always used was to put a big star next to the lead vocal track, so there would be the tape with the words "lead vocal" and this huge star on it. It always made the singer feel special and stroke their ego a bit.

As time marched on, it went from 1-, to 32-, to 48-, to finally having this huge board with all these knobs and controls. It looked complicated, but a 16-track was no different than a 64-track—you just had a lot more options to add this and that, and do overdubs and punch-ins. The process was no different. The flow would be that you would plug a mic into the wall of the studio, that line would go to a mic preamp, and that mic collects a little teeny sound until it gets to the board, where you make it loud and make your adjustments.

Sound-wise, a lot of people don't realize that there is very little difference between a mic and a speaker. You could plug a speaker into a mic jack and still be able to record sound; you could plug a dynamic mic into an output jack and get sound from it. The principle for both is identical. That goes to the heart of what recording really is: the ability to convert something acoustic into something electric.

When you talk, you are producing an acoustic sound wave. Recording is simply converting that acoustic sound wave into an electronic signal by running it through a circuit. It's electrical to acoustical transfer; no more, no less.

So, this mic would go to the preamp, which would boost the signal to get it into something that was strong enough to get it on tape. After a preamp, it would go into the processor or mixer, and that was were you could add highs and lows, and make your tweaks and adjustments to get whatever sound it was you were shooting for. There was no right or wrong; it was just what sounded good. There used to a saying: "Doing it like Count Basie would do it," and that meant: if you liked it, it was good; if you didn't, it was bad.

Basically, it was that simple, and no one would argue over it. I'll get into that a bit more when we talk more about Pink Floyd and Bob Ezrin.

After the preamp and the processor, the signal would pass through what was known as a "bus." It was called a bus just because that is what it did: it would transport, or "bus", the signal where you wanted it to go. You could bus it to one track, or you could bus it to five tracks. It was merely a tool that would ship the signal were you needed it to be. For example, you could use the bass to ship the bass drum to one specific track, or to a mix of sounds on one track. It is all about getting the right sound to the right track.

SC: So, when we talk about great sounding albums, this process is basically what makes them sound great. You could take 10 tracks just to maximize a kick drum, right?

GS: If that is what you wanted to do—and some did—that is correct.

SC: So, great sounding albums took a whole hell of a lot of time to record, produce, mix, and every step along the way?

GS: Yes. It's also what makes the difference between a basic, no-frills demo studio, and The Producer's Workshop or Sunset Sound. With a demo studio, you throw up a couple of mics, and you get what you get.

What I described with the drums was also used in similar fashion on a lot of those great Elton John songs. Bill Schnee and myself would use something we called a "close mic," and it was a little inside joke. The "close mic" was a technique where you would basically put your ear right to the sound source you were trying to capture. Your ear was the mic, and you got close to the sound source to get an idea of what it should sound like.

I always knew when an engineer didn't have a music background and was simply going by the book when they wouldn't actually go into the studio to get close and listen to the instrument being recorded. It is probably one reason I am deaf today, but that's what you had to do—but, it took a toll on your hearing.

SC: You and Pete Townshend.

GS: It wasn't uncommon at the end of the day, when you were recording some albums for someone to say, "Okay, lets call it a day," and you would look at them and go "What?" After a day of recording, your ears would stop picking up high frequencies. It was even worse if the acts you were working with were using cocaine, as we found that those under the influence of coke could not hear high frequencies either, and it made it challenging when it came mixing time. I won't name names, but I can't tell you how many times we would have to go through changes because of that.

We referred to it as "blight," where they would add all of this top-heavy mix. They would come in the next day and listen to the mix, complain about it, and we would always say, "That's where you were last night; how about today we do it straight?"

SC: C'mon, name some names for us.

GS: Nah, I don't want to bust anybody [laughs]. Okay, I will name one: Dick Wagner.

SC: Dick Wagner?

GS: He was Alice Cooper's guitarist with whom I worked. He was trying to launch his solo career. He came in after we recorded with Pink Floyd.

I think Bob Ezrin recommended us, and we were just doing some final stuff. I think we were working for only a week or two to do overdubs or something.

Anyways, I was focused on the job, and this session had all of these people wanting different things and it was pretty chaotic. One of the things that happens a lot in the studio is that the bassist wants his bass louder, or the guitarist wants his part louder—it was always the same. So, I would be working the board and adjusting this and adding that.

By this time, I had learned that part of the job of the engineer was to almost put on a show for the musicians by continually adjusting and fiddling with dials to look as if you were really working some magic. I would sometimes just leave one of the tracks on the console board that the band could see open with nothing on it, and then continually use that track to look like I was always in motion and fiddling with dials.

Remember the story I told earlier about throwing the paper on the floor because I didn't know there was a bunch of coke on it? Well, that happened during the Dick Wagner sessions.

SC: So, Bob Ezrin produced Dick Wagner?

GS: Yeah, I think he got a full producer's credit or something, but for that recording, he was never there, and I never saw him.

SC: So, if the record company hired Bob Ezrin to produce Dick Wagner, they must have really invested a lot of money, thinking he was going to be a big star or something, right?

GS: Oh yeah. They probably lost a ton of money signing him and hiring the production staff, the studios, and the whole bit. He and his band were just blowing money left and right.

SC: I am not familiar with Dick Wagner at all, but do you think, had they not been doing coke and drinking, that they may have been able to record some quality records?

GS: I think so. He was a talented guy with some skill. As I mentioned with Lee Rittenour and some of those other musicians: if you are good enough, and have your head together, there is almost always going to be some role you can fill. Even being a studio musician would pay the bills.

Remember the story I told earlier about the coke in the bag, and the musicians putting their heads in and snorting it? That was actually Dick Wagner and his band. With that going on, how good are you really going to be?

SC: When you said you put on a little show for the musicians by working the mixing board…if you had everything set up perfectly, and didn't need to make adjustments whatsoever, were the musicians disappointed by you not doing anything in the control room and just sitting there looking like you weren't doing your job?

GS: Absolutely. I can tell you a specific story about that.

When I was running the show, I couldn't be working on every track that was being recorded, so from time to time, we would hire people for jobs and projects. One guy we hired was highly recommended, and he came from Motown. He was really a great engineer, but he had this stoic, Abe Lincoln-like look to him, where he just would not show excitement or interest. Once again, he was a great engineer, but lost the gig just because there was a sense of lack of interest or something.

SC: Had he just occasionally looked interested and worked the board a bit more—even if he was doing absolutely nothing to the mix—he would have still had a job?

GS: Probably. He was a good engineer, but it's show business and it is what it is. Another strike against him was that he didn't come from a music background.

What I found was that musicians liked working other musicians, because I could understand the process from top to bottom. As a musician, I could sense when the performer wanted to move faster, or when they wanted to work slower. A non-musician probably would not be as adept at getting a feel for a situation, whereas a guy with a music background would.

It would be like a guy who loves cars and working on cars; he is going to be a better mechanic than a guy who went to the best school but who is just doing it for a job. I was lucky enough that my interest and passion for music was still paying dividends, even though I was working on the other side of the glass. It's a creative thing, and I understood the mindset.

Some engineers or producers would maybe give some musicians crap for going outside and smoking a joint or something, but as a former musician, I always thought if it helped a performer get their head into it, I was able to get a better take or a better overdub because of it. Sometimes, there could be an adversarial relationship between the musicians and the engineers, but in my case, I was able to work with them on their level and almost be one of them during the recording process. Knowing how the creative mind worked, in my case, really helped getting certain things from the performers.

SC: So, we were talking about the studio, and how you got certain sounds and whatnot. You had gotten into some deep specifics about setting up a drum kit to record, and how that was done. When you worked on Ringo's album, was he actually playing any of the drums, or was it pretty much all him handling the vocals and the drumming was all left to Jim Keltner?

GS: For Ringo's album at Sunset Sound we did a full mic setup for Jim Keltner's drums, but for Ringo, we just set up the kick, the snare, and hat cymbal, because that was really all Ringo used anyway. He would wiggle his head back and forth on just this little drum kit.

SC: Even in the studio, Ringo would bob his head like he did on Ed Sullivan and all of the old Beatles film clips?

GS: Yeah, he would do that in the studio when playing drums when he was feeling it. "I'm just a fucking personality" he would always say, but when he was playing drums, even in the studio, he looked just like he did in the concert with the head-bob and other mannerisms and all that.

It's funny though, now when I think of Ringo, the first thing that comes to mind is always his "I'm just a fucking personality" line. He was a great guy, and I was surprised and impressed by his humility. Based on that level of fame, you could expect a certain amount of ego, like you would see with other stars…but he was really down to earth with an honesty and self-effacing style that took me by surprise.

SC: That is something I am not sure a lot of people would know. How was his drum kit setup in the studio for recording?

GS: I think that was just his style and part of what he did that makes him "Ringo." Here is the thing; in the studio, when we were recording, we would get three mics for Ringo, and the full complete mic setup for Jim.

If memory serves, Jim was on the right side of the studio, with Ringo's drum setup to the left. We may have used some of Ringo's stuff, but I am pretty sure that most of the drums on those albums were from Jim Keltner. They may have blended in some of Ringo's tracks, but probably not many.

I remember Richard Perry was typically, "Err, uh, argh, ugh...we're not going to use that." Richard Perry knew what was good, and what wasn't. He wasn't going to stroke someone's ego at the expense of putting out or diluting a good record. Ringo didn't have an ego anyway, so it was probably an easy decision to make.

SC: Earlier, you said that Richard Perry had an amazing ear and amazing talent. Can you elaborate on that?

GS: Richard had a talent for hearing little things in each track, either good or bad, that he could make better. More than that, though, Richard was the best in the business for matching the right song with the right artist, and capturing that song. He knew the song. He could hear the song, and instantly know who would be the best artist to record it.

The "No No Song" was a great example of that, and it became a big hit. Later, he also did a lot of the hits from The Pointer Sisters and other big acts of that time.

SC: That's right; people forget that he had a ton of success as one of the big-time disco producers. He was pretty versatile to be able to produce established pop and rock artists, and then transition into disco and still maintain that level of success.

GS: He was an excellent producer. I learned a lot from him. I probably learned the most from Bob Ezrin, but for sure Richard Perry was a close, close second from the producers I had the pleasure to work with.

SC: Tell us more about the console, and using the console to separate the instruments, and how that helped to make great sound.

GS: Well, as stated earlier, for me, it all started with a good drum track. Once we got that, it was easy, as part of the routine was to add the guitar, the bass, the keyboard or piano, and whatever overdubs you wanted to add.

When you got those parts down, you wanted to add as much separation of those parts as possible, because, ideally, you want to be able to listen to a track and hear each unique part.

For example, early Beatle records had kind of a muddy sound, because they were only using 4-track recorders. Trying to pick up a rhythm guitar part on "I Saw Her Standing There" is not as easy as hearing the guitar parts on Abbey Road, because the technology had improved to where getting separation was much easier. If you listen to Side 2 of Abbey Road, you can hear every individual instrument used, and it's marvelous. That's what makes it a treat to listen to.

As the 70s went on, there was an additional step in the recording process that we started utilizing, and that was integrating processors—or "outboard gear" as we called them. There weren't a lot, but there were a few in the big studios. Nowadays, you have ProTools, Audacity, and programs like that, and all of the almost unlimited options that come with those to adjust the sounds and the tones.

Back then, we didn't have that, so we were fortunate enough to have processors. At the time, it was state of the art, but now, any digital recording program has some type of processor.

The main piece of outboard gear was something known as a "limiter." We used them on the bass more than anything, but working with Pink Floyd, all of the traditional rules of thumb about the recording industry were thrown out the window. There were no boundaries to do whatever was needed to get the best sound.

A limiter was able to keep the signal at a consistent level. Before limiters, if a bass player was really plucking a string on a particular note harder than other strings, you could see the difference in the signal with a huge peak. That presented a challenge to record, because sometimes it may upset the balance, or maybe clash with something the guitar or piano was doing when trying to do the mix.

The limiter was important, because it meant no matter how hard or soft the instrument was being played, it was relayed into the console with a consistent signal, and the louder parts wouldn't become distorted or fuzzy. Each board had a VU meter that would be a visual representation of the sound level signals, and before the limiter, you would listen to a track and see the VU jump in parts.

The limiter changed all that, and, to some extent, enabled an engineer a few more options to "color" the sound. Using the limiter in conjunction with the equalizer opened up a lot of opportunities to get some amazing sound in particular.

What people do not realize, though, was that on some boards, there would only be three options to equalizing a signal. They were highs, lows, and mids, and maybe some types of filters. Then, we got another piece of outboard equipment: a graphic equalizer, which would allow the adjustment of 100 cycles, 500 cycles, or 5K and 10K cycles.

That meant the range of sound you could get, adjust, and enhance was almost unlimited, as opposed to the three previous options of low, medium, and high.

Then, the biggest thing to ever happen to the industry was the advent of the echo units and echo devices. That was huge for us. When I worked at Elektra, they were known for having great echo, and a lot of people don't know it, but even Capitol Records was known for having great echo chambers. The Capitol Records building in LA was using the basement as an echo chamber, and getting that great echo sound. Like singing in the shower, you get that echo, and Capitol Records used their basement to get that great sound.

The way you would originally get echo was to send a signal to a speaker into a room, and they would have different sized rooms, which would give different types of echo. That echo would be caught on one or two mics, which would bring the signal back, and that would produce an echo or delay sound for a track.

Then, a little bit later, we had the first artificial echo. They called them EMTs, and they were these big, clunky units that would sit in the corner, and it was just this huge monstrosity with wires and everything. It wasn't much longer after that the first digital units were starting to be commonplace. They were much smaller and easier to use, and we would refer to them as R2D2s after the Star Wars character that had just came out at that time.

When I worked with Roger Waters, I coined a phrase. When you listen to music, you have two ears, which are, in essence, two speakers—one left and one right. Roger would say on some of the tracks that they may have been using two speakers when they were only getting the result of one speaker. This happened because they weren't separating them, or just sending the same signal to both speakers, with that signal basically becoming one signal for the output, because you became accustomed to just hearing it as one signal.

Once we started splitting the signals and changing the mix to the left, or adding echo to the right signal, it was like a big celebration. It was huge, because then you had so many other options and variations you could use to sweeten a part and add something to a track. When adding those little things to one signal, but sending it to the left and right channels in different forms with different settings, you actually created what I called "the illusion of depth."

Roger loved that phrase, and that happens when you sent an identical signal to a left and right channel, because the output is basically flat. By tweaking the variables and sending the same signal with different echo and different equalization to the left and right channels, it created an aural illusion of depth. Roger loved it, because he thought it was great for setting a mood or getting a feeling of depth to a song. It was basically another option for creativity, as opposed to just working a track "flat," as we started referring to it.

SC: That's interesting. I am not sure you know or realize this, but the follow up to *"The Wall"* was *"The Final Cut,"* and *"The Final Cut"* was made from demos and songs that did not make it onto *"The Wall,"* with David Gilmour only writing one or two songs and Rick Wright not playing on the album after having been fired after *"The Wall."* Gilmour hated it [the album], but Roger Waters actually recorded it with a technique known as "Holophonics," which was developed by a guy named Hugo Zuccarelli.

In *The Final Cut*, you hear a guy walking down an alley, people in a pub, and other cool sound effects. So, your work in developing that "illusion of depth" actually played a role in how *The Final Cut* was recorded, and probably served as inspiration.

GS: Roger really liked being able to get that "illusion of depth," or "full-spectrum audio" I guess some would call it.

When we were recording the phone call portion of *The Wall*, we actually recorded all of that stuff on our own, with that idea of the illusion of depth. We were doing everything from scratch, and custom recording each one of the sounds and segue ways specifically for *The Wall*. We tried to get the most accurate signal and audio capture as possible. For the phone call specifically, most people would be surprised how much work went into trying to accurately reproduce a simple phone call from scratch.

Roger and I spent so much time on all of the sounds…I have some other stories I can get to later. Fortunately, we also captured a lot of cool things by accident and not by design. Roger was so cool, though, because if something didn't work, or something happened, but he liked the sound, and he liked the feel of a sound, we would think about other ways we could use it. We would get creative with how we could potentially work it into the final mix of *The Wall*.

I think it may have been on "Comfortably Numb," where we were using a work vocal as a guide for the acoustic guitar track. If it was the real vocal, it would not have mattered, because it would have synced up on the playback and blended in and maybe even created an extra effect or cool layer of sound.

With a work vocal, it's just a no-frills, dry run through to help build the song. When we were doing this specific take, there was some bleed over from the vocal track onto the guitar track, which meant you could hear the guide vocals on the acoustic track we were trying to record.

However, Roger loved the guitar track, and wanted to somehow use it without having to re-record and asked, "What can we do about it?" Once again, working with Roger was great, because even though we were working on the clock and had a schedule to keep, if he liked an idea and thought it would improve the overall song, that took precedence over deadlines, budget, and everything else.

So, what we did was take the guitar track with the leaked vocal, and then EQ'd it to remove all of the highs. To give a quick background, you can hear the highs from a close distance, but the farther away you are, the less pronounced the highs get. With the lows, it's the exact opposite. A low frequency carries far better than a high, and that's the reason why the kid in the car with the speakers blowing out rap songs with bass and drum seem to carry forever and you can hear them from three blocks away. A low frequency can carry.

So, we cut the highs, and then ran it through another channel, but reversed it. In essence, it was playing backwards, and then EQ'd the track with a subtle echo. Roger loved it. You can hear it with a good quality copy of *The Wall* when listening through headphones. If you listen to the delayed vocals right after the "hello, hello, hello" part, you can hear this otherworldly, creepy tone in the background that gives an extra layer that creates a sense of depth.

That is what makes that album, and some of the others, so interesting. Other acts would come in later, wondering, "How did you get that feel for 'Comfortably Numb'?"

I would just say, "Don't even ask, because I don't have the time to even start."

Roger approved all of the tracks and all of the variables we included on *The Wall*, and he loved it, because you didn't have to throw a track away, and it added to the depth of the song.

SC: Like a collage of sound.

GS: Exactly. Even some of the things that weren't intended to be on there—but sounded good and added something—ended up on the final master mix. That, in my opinion, is what makes *The Wall* the great, classic album it is.

You could hear it over and over again, and still pick up little things you never noticed before. Instead of a song being a guitar part and a vocal part, it became something bigger, and the vocal track ended up just being the sum of a part that was something brilliant. Then, you had the guys on acid who thought they were hallucinating and hearing something no one else had heard before, which took it all to another level entirely.

SC: When you are working next to Roger Waters, making great money, having the flexibility and the sky's-the-limit attitude to do whatever you want with one of rock's greatest visionaries, it must have been a lot of fun and one hell of a ride, right?

GS: It was a thrill, without question.

It was 20 hours on and 4 hours off, though, so it was also a very tiring and rigorous schedule to keep up for months on end, and it was work. However, it wasn't about the money. It was the one time in my life—and maybe the only time in my life—where money and career didn't even enter the equation or the thought process. That was the thing; when I took the job, they wanted someone who would get as invested in the project as they were, and that is why I got hired.

Honestly, at that time, I really wasn't even a Pink Floyd fan. I didn't have any of their records, and would change the station if a song of theirs came on the radio. When I got the job, I wasn't starry-eyed or star-struck at all—not like I was with John Lennon and Ringo.

With Lennon, I was in a constant state of just being awestruck by being in the same room as the guy. With Pink Floyd and Roger Waters, it was just almost a case of "another job dealing with some English guys." In the end, it became a fantastic working relationship.

SC: How had your attitude changed when you were done with the project? After working with him and sitting side by side, did you think, "There was a lot more to this guy then I had thought"?

GS: Once I heard *The Wall* from beginning to end, and again at the release party we all attended, it hit me, and I realized how talented Waters is, and I was in awe of him. I was like, "Did this really happen? Did I really work with this guy on this album?" It was like winning the lottery once it was released, and had the sales, recognition, and acclaim *The Wall* received.

SC: And now, with time, Roger Waters may not be quite the towering figure that John Lennon was, but, without question, he is one of the most iconic and legendary rock personalities.

GS: He is a big-time icon, and he is a very talented man. I saw him live last time he came to LA, and tried to get in touch with him, but at some point, the fame and level of talent means it's virtually impossible to reach out to them, because of their management companies and handlers and all that stuff. That is the business and going back to my experience with Tom Petty's management company it is something to be expected.

If I ever can get back in touch, it would be a great to sit down and talk with him again. I would even like to get back with Bob Ezrin again.

I'd like to make him feel guilty about me not getting my album credit.

SC: Maybe we could use it as leverage to get a sit down interview with him. Do you think if you were able to get back in touch with Bob, he would sit down with us for an interview? Would he remember you, the story, and make a future interview viable?

GS: It's one hundred-percent doable. He would remember me, for sure. I mean, he chose me, specifically, to be the guy to guard *The Wall* master tapes that made him an extra $2 million dollars. I think that carries some clout, and something you wouldn't forget.

He came to me a year or so after *The Wall*, when he came back from London. He was apologetic, and actually approached me with the subject of the missing credit. I guarantee you he remembers it.

SC: To tie *The Wall* back to Lennon and then to The Beatles, without The Beatles assuming studio control, and getting the power to control everything they recorded and how it was recorded, would they have ever been able to create *The Wall?*

GS: The Beatles were the first to be given full control and carte blanche to do whatever they wanted in the studio. It is safe to say that, without them, there would not have been the big-production albums.

As I look back, sadly, I think *The Wall* was probably the last of the big-production albums.

It wasn't unlike the movie industry in the heyday of Hollywood. The Wizard of Oz was this grand spectacle that everyone was anxious to see. *The Wall*, *Rumours*, *Aja*, and other albums of that stature were—in my opinion—the last of a fantastic era of music.

Everything after that began to get progressively cheaper and more cookie-cutter, I guess you could say. To tie it back again to John Lennon, it was one of the reasons he was so angry about *The Yellow Submarine* movie. I think he had a higher vision about what it should be, and when the studio and the powers that be told him no and cut corners on it, it probably left a bad taste is his mouth.

At that point, as both a musician and an engineer, and having been ripped off so many times here and there, and the litany of broken promises that happened to me personally… and then to see that John Lennon went through, and was going through the same type of issues, kind of left me totally disillusioned with the business. Then, with each subsequent issue getting progressively worse, I had enough, and thus, ended my career in music and that chapter of my life working with rock and roll legends.

ALL IN ALL IT'S JUST ANOTHER BRICK...

Printed in Great Britain
by Amazon.co.uk, Ltd.,
Marston Gate.